D0916924

HANDBOOK OF
SECRET ORGANIZATIONS

Handbook of
Secret Organizations

WILLIAM J. WHALEN

THE BRUCE PUBLISHING COMPANY / *Milwaukee*

By the same author:

Separated Brethren
Christianity and American Freemasonry
Christian Family Finance
Catholics on Campus
Armageddon Around the Corner
Faiths for the Few
The Latter-day Saints in the Modern Day World
Effective Publications for Colleges and Universities
  (with Kelvin J. Arden)

Library of Congress Catalog Card Number: 66–26658

© 1966 THE BRUCE PUBLISHING COMPANY
MADE IN THE UNITED STATES OF AMERICA

(Second printing — 1967)

Preface

This handbook seeks to present basic current information about some forty-five major secret organizations in the United States along with information about dozens of smaller organizations.

Our definition of secret organization includes the criterion of a secret ritual and initiation ceremony. Some organizations display elements of secrecy but do not work a secret ritual, administer oaths, or exclude outsiders from attending regular meetings. For example, the John Birch society refuses to disclose its membership but has no secret ritual. Such organizations have been excluded.

The exclusion of certain other organizations should be explained. B'nai B'rith, the Jewish fraternal order, has dropped its secrecy and no longer qualifies as a secret organization. We have not attempted in this study to describe secret political societies such as the Communist Party; anyone interested in the secret aspects of Communism may consult a library of literature on this subject.

We debated whether to include the Church of Jesus Christ of Latter-day Saints — the Mormons — as a secret organization. The Mormon Church works secret rituals, the endowment ceremony, in temples which are closed to all non-Mormons and even to those Mormons who fail to meet certain personal requirements. These temple rites have obviously been patterned after the Masonic ritual which fascinated Joseph Smith, Brigham Young, and other Mormon leaders in the Nauvoo, Illinois, lodge. They include passwords, secret grips, robes, oaths, and ritualistic playlets. We finally decided to leave the Mormon Church out of this handbook because it is more a religious denomination than a lodge or fraternity. We should note, however, that its temple secrecy has probably contributed to its *esprit de corps* and to its success in winning converts in recent years.

Everyone engaged in research in the field of secret organizations must express a debt of gratitude to the *Cyclopaedia of Fraternities* edited by Albert C. Stevens and published in 1907. Other studies which have provided valuable information and insights are the *Dictionary of Secret and Other Societies* by Arthur Preuss (1924) and the *Handbook of Organizations* by Theodore Graebner (1948). These volumes are now out of print.

We wish to thank the officers of many of the organizations described in this handbook for cooperating by returning the author's questionnaire and furnishing additional factual information about the history, goals, and activities of their groups.

Special thanks must go to the Rev. Philip H. Lochhaas, director of the Commission on Fraternal Organizations of the Lutheran Church-Missouri Synod, who reviewed the manuscript and offered wise and informed comments. My wife also assisted in the preparation of the book by her suggestions and encouragement. Mrs. Leslie Jones typed the manuscript.

We hope that this handbook will be of particular interest to priests and ministers concerned about dual membership in the Church and in a secret society. For many religious denominations this remains a serious problem.

W.J.W.

March 15, 1966
Lafayette, Indiana

Contents

HANDBOOK OF
SECRET ORGANIZATIONS

PART I

The World of Secret Organizations

From primitive times to the present day men and women have sworn the solemn oaths, preserved the secrets, and worked the rituals of secret societies. Ancients petitioned to discover the arcana of the mystery religions of the Mediterranean world. The Knights Templar, Gnostics, Illuminati, and Carbonari practiced their rites and administered their oaths shielded from the profane. In almost every culture from the Chinese to the Eskimo and from the South Seas to the African village men have banded together in secret societies.

In numbers of such societies and in membership no nation has surpassed the United States. Although competition from other recreational activities has hurt lodge attendance, we estimate that at least 15,000,000 American men and women belong to one or more secret organizations. Noel Gist has called the secret society "one of the major patterns of American civilization" and it would be difficult or impossible to understand many aspects of American life without considering the role played by these societies.

Can you understand the civil rights movement without examining the influence of the Ku Klux Klan of the 1920's as well as the contemporary versions of the Klan in several Southern states? Can you form an accurate picture of the American college campus without taking a look at the fraternity-sorority system? Can you analyze the values of middle-class whites without knowing something about the Masonic lodges, the Shrine, or the Elks, Moose, and Eagles? Can you describe organized crime in this country if you ignore the Mafia? Can you characterize the social patterns of the Negro community without including the Negro lodges?

Secret societies have played and are playing a significant role in American life. This is true not only of such societies as the Know Nothings, Freemasonry, the Knights of Labor, and the Ku Klux Klan, but of the dozens of other secret organizations. The values they try to inculcate, the fellowship they foster, the social and political changes they instigate or block affect the entire nation.

Most of these societies follow the pattern set by Masonry in the eighteenth century. Their degree systems, passwords, grips, and regalia usually display the influence of the oldest and largest fraternity. Only a few, such as the National Grange and the Catholic Order of Foresters, admit men and women on an equal basis; most secret organizations initiate members of one sex. Almost all the major American lodges except the Knights of Columbus refuse to initiate Negroes.

At the start of the nineteenth century only a few thousand Americans belonged to secret societies. These included about 3000 Freemasons, 600 members of Tammany, and a few Phi Beta Kappas. Agitation against Masonry began in 1826 with the Morgan affair and slowed the growth of other secret societies as well for several decades. Between 1800 and 1900 some 600 secret societies were founded in the United States but most of these have disappeared. Masonry remains by far the largest secret organization; with 4,200,000 members the Craft enrolls about one out of every dozen adult males in this country. Yet even this membership total fell short of the 5,000,000 members claimed by the Ku Klux Klan in the middle 1920's.

Among the scores of active secret organizations in the United States we can categorize all but a few in several major classifications. The benevolent societies such as Freemasonry and Odd Fellowship try to assist members and their families in times of distress. Yet the member has no absolute claims on the beneficence of the order. The various insurance societies put this aid on a *quid pro quo* basis with premiums and stipulated insurance benefits; in this category we would include the Foresters, Woodmen, Royal Arcanum, etc. They combine the rituals of the lodge with the hard facts of actuarial tables.

College fraternities and sororities make up another category of secret society as do the various honor and professional societies which go back in purpose to Phi Beta Kappa.

The "animal" lodges — Elks, Moose, and Eagles — claim the allegiance of 3,000,000 men and offer a program which is primarily social and convivial but which also includes elements of service to the community. Both the Moose and Eagles have de-emphasized ritualism in recent years.

Members of the major lodges often join the satellite "fun" organizations such as the Shrine, Grotto, Tall Cedars of Lebanon, or Dramatic Order Knights of Khorassan. Auxiliaries such as the Eastern Star and the Rebekah lodges initiate both male members of the parent organization and their female relatives.

Religion provides a major motivation for those who join the Knights of Columbus, the Loyal Orange Institution, and the Knights of Malta. Nationality is a determinant of membership for such lodges as the Ancient Order of Hibernians.

The National Grange is the largest of the occupational secret societies but others have been organized for policemen, hardware dealers, lumbermen, etc. The lumbermen's fraternity is known as the International Concatenated Order of Hoo Hoo; it convenes only during the ninth month, elects nine top officers, and charges initiates $9.99.

Negroes have organized counterparts of the Masons, Scottish and York rites, Shrine, Eastern Star, Odd Fellows, Knights of Pythias, and Elks and have founded several lodges of their own. Men and women interested in the occult may join Theosophical or Rosicrucian lodges.

Some categories of secret societies have been on the decline for several decades. These include the total abstinence societies such as the Good Templars and the nativist groups such as the Junior Order United American Mechanics and the Sons and Daughters of Liberty.

Secret societies display many common elements. For example, the society will usually divide initiation into successive stages or degrees. The Master Mason who has completed the third degree of the Blue Lodge may elect to continue in the twenty-nine degrees of the Scottish rite or the degrees of the York rite. The Odd Fellows work seven degrees and the Knights of Columbus offer four.

Members ballot on the acceptability of those who apply to join their ranks. In some societies a single blackball will disqualify an applicant while in others some larger number or percentage of voting members is required before an applicant is turned down. Members seldom need to explain their blackball so that changes in the social composition of single-blackball lodges will come late if ever; any individual can blackball applicants of any race or religion he disdains.

Secret organizations often feel a need to appeal to antiquity. Speculative Freemasonry, which dates from 1717, tells initiates that the Craft began in the days of the building of King Solomon's temple. Even societies with histories which began during the lifetimes of living members try to establish links with the dim past.

Sharp distinctions are drawn between those who belong to the secret society and those who stand outside its walls. Masons refer to non-Masons as "profanes"; fraternity men call the independents "Barbarians" or worse; Klansmen identify those outside the Invisible Empire as "aliens." The new member is given to understand that he is an unworthy supplicant knocking at the door of the storehouse of wisdom and truth.

Ritualistic material is typically drawn from the Bible or from legends such as that of Robin Hood, the American Indian, or Damon and Pythias. The candidate assumes the role of a wayfarer, stranger, pilgrim, intruder, paleface, seeker of light, alien. He is introduced to the secret society, tested, given certain secrets such as the password and grip, and asked to swear a solemn oath that he will preserve these secrets and live a good life. In some of the older societies the symbolic penalty for violating this oath is no less than death or horrible mutilation while in other societies the penalty is nothing more than expulsion from the order.

The initiation rite, usually based on the Masonic model, follows a familiar form. An officer of the lodge questions the candidate regarding his belief in a Supreme Being (almost all lodges set this membership qualification) and his willingness to assume the obligations of the society. He is prepared for the ceremony itself by changing from street clothes to a special garment or robe. He is often blindfolded.

The conductor raps on the door of the lodge room and in a moment he and the candidate(s) are admitted to the inner sanctum. For the next hour or so the candidate is marched around the lodge room, instructed in the noble principles of the lodge, questioned, and perhaps subjected to various obstacles and tests of courage. In the third degree of Masonry he undergoes a ritualistic death and resurrection. Finally he swears an oath or recites a pledge which is usually administered on the Bible.

The secret society employs symbolism to express its teachings: the all-seeing eye, working tools of some occupation, anchor, star, the points of the compass, altar, cross. Different colors stand for virtues or degrees.

For some of the older lodges the main activity of the

lodge is the initiation of new members. Sometimes only one candidate at a time may be inducted which means that numerous degree sessions must be scheduled by large lodges. Officers and members of the degree team must spend hours memorizing their lines in the initiation playlets.

The monotony of this ritualistic activity and the competition for a share in the lodge member's leisure hours have cut into attendance at lodge meetings. Far more recreational outlets beckon to the lodge member today than in the early years of this century: television, bowling and golf, spectator sports, motion pictures, country clubs, service clubs such as Rotary and Lions, automobile, hobbies. Family recreation, church clubs, and adult education programs also draw the brother or sister away from frequent lodge attendance. Lodges with 500 members may be able to attract only forty or fifty members for an initiation or business meeting although attendance may be higher for a banquet, smoker, card party, or dance.

Some lodges have enjoyed membership spurts in recent years because of local situations. In the South, for example, the Elks have won many new members since public swimming pools have been desegregated. Again, those lodges which operate bars enroll thirsty members in dry areas or in towns where bars are generally closed on Sunday.

During the anti-Masonic agitation of the early nineteenth century many mainline Protestant denominations and preachers opposed lodge membership. Today the major Protestant denominations raise no serious objection to lodge membership. This is not true of all churches. The Lutheran Church-Missouri Synod, Wisconsin Evangelical Lutheran Synod, Christian Reformed Church, Church of the Brethren, Mennonite churches, Quakers, Salvation Army, Assemblies of God, Church of the Nazarene, Seventh-Day Adventist Church, Wesleyan and Free Methodist churches, Orthodox Presbyterian Church, Reformed Presbyterian Church, and many Holiness bodies forbid or discourage lodge affiliation. These Protestants object to the religious character of the lodge and the oaths demanded of initiates.

Opposition to Freemasonry has stiffened among Eastern Orthodox in recent years although not every Orthodox body forbids such membership. The Church of Jesus Christ of Latter-day Saints (Mormons) and Jehovah's Witnesses also frown on secret societies such as Masonry.

The Roman Catholic Church excommunicates members who enter the Masonic lodge; the first such papal ban was issued in 1738 and it has been confirmed by seven succeeding popes. The Catholic Church also forbids membership in Masonic auxiliaries such as the Order of the Eastern Star, DeMolay, Job's Daughters, and Rainbow Girls. Catholic men who join the Odd Fellows or Knights of Pythias are denied the sacraments but are not excommunicated; under certain conditions they may maintain nominal membership in these two lodges. Catholics have been dissuaded from joining the Good Templars and the Rosicrucians (AMORC). They are barred from the Loyal Orange Institution and the Knights of Malta by the membership qualifications and are rarely invited to join the Ku Klux Klan.

With millions of members, tens of millions of dollars in assets and property, and billions of dollars' worth of insurance in force the secret societies in this country are not likely to disappear in the near future. During affluent times they lose few members for nonpayment of dues although during the Depression in the 1930's millions of lodgemen dropped their memberships. Many men and women no doubt join a secret society, lose interest, but continue to pay dues; they may hold insurance policies which they do not wish to surrender or may simply prefer to pay a few dollars a year in dues rather than make enemies among the active brethren by resigning.

Gerald George has observed: "A lingering look into the working of the various orders and lodges around the country discloses among other things, that many are forming into middle-class country clubs, replete with luxurious bars, swimming pools, and top-flight entertainment." He adds: "Many, in effect, have become family fraternities rather than places for men only. There is a discernible de-emphasis on ritual and regalia and a growing emphasis in many places on participation in civic affairs, along with a continuing interest in doing good works" (*National Observer*, Feb. 21, 1966, p. 22).

Secret societies have had difficulty getting active participation in ritual work and getting new blood from the ranks of the diploma elite. Young business and professional men sometimes see no particular advantage in lodge affiliation.

Yet many of the established secret societies continue to grow. They are the fittest survivors among the hundreds founded during the nineteenth century and presumably still incorporate elements which contributed to their success. They must be meeting the needs of those millions of men and women who remain loyal and whose example induces others to knock on the lodge room door seeking admission. As such these secret organizations deserve examination by anyone concerned about the major forces in our national life.

PART II

Acacia

On forty-eight college campuses Master Masons, the sons and brothers of Masons, and young men recommended by two Masons may join chapters of Acacia fraternity. Officially the fraternity does not come under the jurisdiction of any state grand lodge of Masons but the closest ties of common ideals and objectives unite the fraternity and the Masonic lodges.

Fourteen Master Masons founded the first Acacia chapter at the University of Michigan in 1904. They chose the name "Acacia" to emphasize their Masonic affiliation. In Freemasonry the acacia symbolizes immortality; Masons often place a sprig of acacia on the coffin of a deceased brother.

An article in the November, 1965, issue of the *New Age* reports that Acacia "selected its members from Master Masons who were students of a college or university, who were both serious and clubable and who were determined to keep their fraternity home free from the college fraternity vices of drinking, gambling, and wenching" (p. 15).

The preamble to the constitution of the founding chapter states: "We, Master Masons, firmly believing that the principles of Ancient Free Masonry are worthy of most careful cultivation among university brothers, do hereby adopt this constitution for the purpose of uniting us in closer friendship and to more effectively inculcate Masonic principles in Master Masons of the University of Michigan."

Since its founding the membership requirements have been modified but the basic Masonic orientation of Acacia fraternity has never changed.

Membership was opened in 1933 to young men who

were not themselves Master Masons. It had become increasingly difficult to fill Acacia houses with men who had already received their Masonic degrees since many college freshmen were only eighteen or nineteen years old. The sons and brothers of Freemasons were now to be admitted as well as men who could obtain the recommendation of two Master Masons. One of the latter two had to be an Acacian himself. A further stipulation was made that no one could be initiated who was "an adherent of any creed or organization which seeks to restrain its members from affiliation with Masonic organizations."

This later "adherent" clause was dropped in 1960 mainly because Acacia was coming under attack on certain campuses for its alleged discriminatory policies. In its place the fraternity added a requirement that all pledges must receive adequate instruction in the ideals and culture of Freemasonry as well as in the historic relationship that has existed between Masonry and Acacia.

Before this constitutional change it was obvious that an Acacia chapter which knowingly pledged a Roman Catholic or Missouri Synod Lutheran or member of any other denomination which forbade or discouraged Masonic membership was violating both the letter and spirit of the fraternity's laws. Since 1960 it has become technically possible for a chapter of Acacia to initiate a Roman Catholic whose father or brother is a Master Mason or who can present the recommendation of two Master Masons. Like all pledges he would receive specific instruction in the philosophy of Freemasonry as a prerequisite to initiation.

May a Catholic pledge Acacia? The answer given by Church spokesmen is a clear "no"; this prohibition has been re-emphasized in recent years by the National Association of Newman Chaplains.

The prohibition of membership in Masonry by the

Catholic Church extends also to the various auxiliaries of Masonry such as the Eastern Star, Job's Daughters, DeMolay, Rainbow Girls, and Acacia. The Church cannot allow her sons to become involved in a fraternity whose history, ideals, objectives, and spirit are thoroughly Masonic.

Acacians sometimes maintain that they have no formal ties with the Masonic lodge. This is true but it is also true that Masonry consists essentially in only the three Blue Lodge degrees plus the Royal Arch. There is no formal Masonic approval of even such obviously Masonic-inspired organizations as the Shrine, the Eastern Star, the Grotto. Acacia, like these other auxiliaries, promotes and fosters the principles of Freemasonry which stand in contradiction to those of the Catholic Church. The national governing board of the fraternity is composed exclusively of 32nd- and 33rd-degree Masons.

Catholics who attempt to pledge Acacia subject themselves to automatic excommunication. Should they proceed with their initiation they will find themselves curiosities in a Masonic fraternity and a scandal to their fellow Catholic students. Without disparaging Acacia we could state that this particular fraternity offers nothing which the Catholic college student could not discover in campus fraternities to which the Church raises no objection.

Since Negroes cannot join white Masonic lodges and since the Prince Hall lodges are considered clandestine by the white grand lodges, no Negro can qualify for initiation into Acacia, as a Master Mason, or the son and brother of a Mason. None has ever been recommended for initiation by two Masons.

Acacia belongs to the National Interfraternity Council. Since its founding it has initiated more than 22,000 members. No officers of the fraternity seem to want to tamper with the special relationship of Acacia to the Masonic system; they do wish to escape censure by college administrators because they are believed to discriminate against Catholics.

(See **Fraternities, College**)

Order of Ahepa

Six Americans of Greek ancestry founded the Order of Ahepa in Atlanta, Georgia, in 1922. The name is an acrostic derived from American Hellenic Educational Progressive Association. It is a secret fraternal organization which is both nonpolitical and nonsectarian.

Most of the members of the Order are of Greek nationality but the late President Franklin D. Roosevelt became a member of Ahepa while governor of New York, former President Harry S. Truman retains his membership, and a number of non-Greeks have been initiated. Only citizens of the United States or Canada or those who have declared their intention to become citizens may join the lodge.

Ahepa promotes good citizenship, fellowship, an understanding of Hellenism and Hellenic culture, mutual benevolence, and education. It has made substantial contributions to war and disaster victims in the United States and Greece. Ahepa Hall for Boys and the Ahepa School at St. Basil's Academy in Garrison, New York, were donated by the Order.

The Supreme Lodge, which maintains headquarters in Washington, D. C., governs 430 local chapters in forty-nine states and Canada.

Order of the Alhambra

If Masons can wear fezzes and pretend they are Moslems

as Nobles of the Mystic Shrine, Catholics should enjoy the same advantages — or so reasoned the founders of the Order of the Alhambra in 1904. They invented an order obviously patterned after the Shrine and announced that membership was open only to 3rd- and 4th-degree Knights of Columbus.

Had the Knights of Columbus sanctioned this "Catholic Shrine," the Order of the Alhambra might have grown to sizable proportions but such approval was never forthcoming. Today the Alhambra states that membership invitations are "freely extended to Catholic men in every walk of life who are a credit to their Church and their Country."

The Order was named after the citadel which overlooks Granada and which served as the residence of the Moorish kings in Spain. Here the Moors surrendered to Ferdinand and Isabella in 1492 after occupying Spain for hundreds of years. The emblem of the Order is the tower of Castile surmounting the Moslem crescent.

Each chapter or Caravan of the Order of the Alhambra must hold at least four social meetings a year and sponsor one religious activity. Besides its primary social objective the Order marks spots of historical interest in the history of the Catholic Church in North America. The Alhambra Charity and Catholic Education fund provides financial help to train special teachers of the retarded and handicapped under Catholic auspices.

Among its 13,500 members the Order of the Alhambra claims "Cardinals, Archbishops, Bishops and many Monsignori and Priests." Membership is by invitation only and new candidates must be approved by all other members of a Caravan. The Caravan elects a group of officers known as the Grand Divan and headed by a Grand Commander. A national Supreme Divan sets the rules and regulations of the Order. The monthly magazine is called the *Muezzin*.

The initiation ceremony depicts the deliverance of Christian Spain from the Moors. Since the ceremony demands elaborate equipment and costumes most neophytes go to a central location where one of the larger Caravans conducts the rite. The national headquarters in Baltimore also rents paraphernalia to local Caravans who may wish to conduct an initiation.

Order of Amaranth

The Masons who invented the Order of Amaranth intended it to be the 3rd and highest degree in a Masonic Rite of Adoption. The 1st degree would be the successful Order of the Eastern Star and the 2nd would be a degree known as that of Queen of the South. In this way the ladies of the Eastern Star could relieve the boredom of working the same one degree over and over and could aspire to additional degrees even as the Masons continued in the Scottish and York rites.

But the scheme for a three-degree Rite of Adoption was flatly rejected by the officials of the Eastern Star. The Order of Amaranth was launched as an independent order and without Eastern Star blessing has achieved a membership of about 85,000.

A Royal and Exalted Order of the Amaranth was said to have been created by Queen Christina of Sweden in 1653. It had no connection with the Order of Amaranth founded in New York City on June 14, 1873, by J. B. Taylor.

Later the ritual was improved by Robert Macoy, the Masonic publisher. Until 1921 only members of the Eastern Star could apply for membership in the Order of Amaranth; since then membership has been open to Masons and their wives, mothers, daughters, widows, and sisters.

At least one Mason must be present at every initiation. The landmarks of this rite include "A belief in the existence of a Supreme Being, who will punish the violation of a solemn pledge." The Order also believes "That a covenant of secrecy, voluntarily assumed, is perpetual; from the force of such obligation there is no release."

The initiation follows the usual pattern of such organizations. The candidate receives instruction in the precepts of the Order, washes her hands, marches about the lodge room, eats a bit of bread and salt which are considered the "sacred emblems," kneels and is tapped with a sword on both shoulders by the Royal Matron, and receives a wreath on her head. The assembled members of the Order sing a selection of Christian hymns during the initiation as well as a verse of *Home, Sweet Home*. The initiation for a Master Mason differs in certain respects.

The Order is governed by a supreme council which controls the regional grand courts and the subordinate local lodges.

(See **Eastern Star**)

Catholic Order of Foresters

A small group of Catholic men founded the Catholic Order of Foresters in Holy Family parish in Chicago in 1883. Like other versions of the Foresters they modeled their ritual on the legend of Robin Hood with some specifically religious additions.

Until 1952 the COF remained a typical male fraternal order but in that year it opened its membership to women. Today the Order enrolls men and women from the day of their birth to mature years. It calls itself "A society for the Catholic family."

Up to the age of six, boys and girls are enrolled as Rangers; from seven to fifteen and a half they are known as Forest Rangers; and thereafter as Foresters. The Catholic Order of Foresters reports 191,000 adult and juvenile members. It will initiate Negroes who are members of the Catholic faith.

Subordinate courts or chapters are organized in a parish or geographical area. They are grouped in state or provincial (for Canada) courts. The High Court consists of the chairman of the board, the High Chief Ranger, the Vice High Chief Ranger, the High Secretary, the High Treasurer, and ten Trustees. The COF operates as a legal reserve fraternal life insurance society. Since its founding it has paid more than $140,000,000 to members and their beneficiaries.

The largest COF membership will be found in Wisconsin, Illinois, Minnesota, and Ohio. It counts 6000 members in Canada. In 1965 there were 1170 courts in the United States and 101 in Canada.

The Catholic Order of Foresters absorbed the 4600-member Catholic Central Union in 1965 which had enrolled Catholics of Czech nationality.

(See **Foresters**)

Catholic Workman

A group of Czech Catholics headed by Father John Rynda founded the Katolicy Delnik in 1891. This fraternal life beneficiary association is now known as the Catholic Workman.

The founders met in St. Paul to organize the new association which would not only promote the spiritual and social welfare of the members but help widows and orphans of deceased members. They modeled their organization after the Catholic Knights of America.

D

Most of the branches in the sixteen states in which it operates can be found in Czech parishes. The 1965 membership was 19,000. Headquarters are in New Prague, Minnesota. Since its founding the Catholic Workman has paid benefits totaling more than $6,000,000.

Order of DeMolay

Serving as a recruiting ground for the Masonic lodges, the Order of DeMolay enrolls boys between the ages of fourteen and twenty-one. They need not be sons of Masons but are expected to have some Masonic relative or background. At the time of their initiation 55 percent of the boys joining DeMolay have fathers who are not Masons, according to the January, 1966 issue of the *New Age*. An estimated 65 percent of all DeMolays eventually seek admission to Freemasonry.

Some Masons observed the declining interest in Freemasonry on the part of the more promising young men of the nation many decades ago. One such observer was a Scottish rite Mason, Frank S. Land of Kansas City, whose interest in helping young men become better citizens was coupled with a concern for the future of Freemasonry. Land founded the Order of DeMolay with nine boys in 1919.

Each chapter of DeMolay must be sponsored and supervised by a recognized Masonic organization such as a Blue Lodge, Scottish rite body, York rite body, or Shrine Temple. The Supreme Council of DeMolay includes seventy-five prominent Masons and all the executives at its Kansas City headquarters are Scottish rite Masons.

Since its founding DeMolay claims to have initiated nearly 3,000,000 young men; of these an estimated 40,000 have become Protestant ministers. The present membership is approximately 165,000 boys.

In one Eastern state a survey by the national DeMolay headquarters reported that 82 percent of all men joining the Masonic lodge during a five-year period had been members of DeMolay. More than 17,000 former DeMolays have become Worshipful Masters of Blue Lodges in this country.

When members reach the age of twenty-one they become Senior DeMolays. To induce them to join a Masonic lodge they are told that they cannot attend DeMolay functions unless they do join a lodge. Senior DeMolays include five United States senators, Walt Disney, Olympic star Bob Mathias, writer John Steinbeck, broadcaster John Cameron Swayze, screen stars Van Johnson, Fred MacMurray, and Bob Cummings.

As patron and namesake of the organization Land chose the last Grand Master of the Knights Templar, Jacques DeMolay. He headed the powerful medieval order of soldier-monks who fought the Moslems for the Holy Land. The pope approved the Knights Templar in 1128 and the members lived under a rule drawn up by St. Bernard which included the vows of poverty, chastity, and obedience.

By the time DeMolay became Grand Master the Order had amassed great wealth and power. Pope Clement V summoned DeMolay to come to France from Cyprus to answer charges brought against the Order. These charges included those of blasphemy, heresy, and homosexuality. While the pope was investigating the Order which was under his jurisdiction, Philip the Fair, king of France, ordered the arrest of all the Templars in his domain on October 13, 1307. DeMolay was held in prison for seven years and burned at the stake on March 14, 1314. The Order was disbanded and most of its property was turned over to the rival Knights of St. John of Jerusalem.

Each DeMolay chapter must have an advisory council of

Masons and an advisor or "Dad." The officers of the chapter themselves include the master councilor, senior and junior councilors, senior and junior deacons, senior and junior stewards, orator, chaplain, marshal, scribe, treasurer, almoner, standard bearer, seven preceptors, and sentinel.

The Order works two degrees, the Initiatory degree and the DeMolay degree. The ritual, composed by Frank Marshall who was a newspaperman in Kansas City, is closed to nonmembers. Religious features in the ritual include the prayers of the chaplain, the open Bible on the altar, and familiar hymns such as *Abide With Me, Just as I Am,* and *Nearer, My God, to Thee.*

The Order administers a typical obligation to the candidates for initiation; after the obligation they are required to kiss the Bible. As part of the ritual the senior deacon takes the Crown of Youth and conducts the candidates to the seven preceptors. Each of them places a jewel in the crown; the seven precepts of the Order are filial love, reverence for God, courtesy, comradeship, fidelity, cleanness, and patriotism. As the second jewel is placed into the crown the preceptor explains in part: "My comrades, in our chapter we teach no religious creed. Your religious opinions are your own. But we do earnestly enjoin upon you the sacredness of faith, the beauty of an humble reliance on the goodness of God."

The DeMolay degree dramatizes the trial and death of Jacques DeMolay. The Order provides a ritual for a memorial service for the dead and a funeral service. The mourners and survivors are assured that the dead who have lived according to the precepts of the Order of DeMolay are enjoying the joys of eternal life.

Local chapters sponsor a number of projects such as a teen-age safety campaign, anti-Communism, vocational guidance program, blood donation, antinarcotics, and oratorical contest.

For any Catholic boy to enter the Order of DeMolay, which is clearly a novitiate of the Masonic lodge, would be to gravely compromise his religious faith. The prohibition against membership in the Masonic lodge extends also to such Masonic auxiliaries as the Order of DeMolay.

Druids
(United Ancient Order of Druids)

The ancient Celtic religion of the Druids forms the framework for the ritual and philosophy of the modern lodge of Druids. The first lodge of Druids was said to have been organized in London in 1771 and transplanted to the United States in 1830.

The original Druids served as priests and teachers to the inhabitants of the British Isles and Gaul; they were skilled in magic and astrology and were assisted by sorceresses. The Druids taught a belief in a Supreme Power, usually identified with the sun. Another basic belief was in the immortality of the soul; the Druids believed that at death the soul passed into the body of a newborn baby.

Not much is known about specified Druidic practices. They are thought to have worshiped outdoors near sacred oak trees and to have venerated the mistletoe. Some archaeologists have suggested that the stone dolmens in England were used by them as altars but others dispute this theory. Julius Caesar nearly exterminated the Druids when he conquered Britain but the religion survived in isolated parts of the island until Christianity replaced it in the fourth and fifth centuries.

The modern lodge of Druids, like the original religion, is pure paganism. A circular published by the Druids of California and Nevada states: "The Druids of today confine themselves to the moral, fraternal, patriotic and benevolent philosophy exemplified by the Druids of old. Their teachings and principles are derived from ancient Druidism, founded on reason and sound morality." Unlike some lodges the United Ancient Order of Druids makes no pretense that it is Christian; in fact it implies that the religion of the Druids is not only older but superior to Christianity.

The same pamphlet states: "The greatest of all Druidic teachers was Merlin, and his Seven Precepts are considered as a moral way of life, the finest moral virtues ever laid down for the guidance of man." These precepts are: (1) Labor diligently to acquire knowledge for it is power; (2) When in authority decide reasonably, for thine authority may cease; (3) Bear with fortitude the ills of life, remembering that no mortal sorrow is perpetual; (4) Love virtue — for it bringeth peace; (5) Abhor vice — for it bringeth evil upon all; (6) Obey those in authority in all just things, that virtue may be exalted; and (7) Cultivate the social virtues, so shalt thou be beloved by all men.

The United Ancient Order of Druids states as its purposes:

> The objects of the Order are to unite men together, irrespective of nationality, for mutual protection to cultivate the social virtues, provide for the widows and orphans of deceased members, help members in time of sickness and adversity, encourage business, foster among its members the spirit of fraternity and good fellowship, and above all to learn to respect the conscientious beliefs and feelings of one's fellow men.

This lodge works three degrees: Ovate, Bard, and Druid. A candidate who is admitted to the Order becomes a member of a local lodge known as a Grove. Women may enter a parallel order known as the Circle which is also open to male Druids. Officers of a Grove as well as past officers may join the Chapter which is the fun organization of the UAOD.

The authors of *The Story of Druidism* admit "Although Druidism is neither a religious or political organization, the Druids do partake in a measure of the nature of both. Druidism is not a religion, but the Druids profess a religious Faith, as manifested, in their belief in the Almighty God, and the Immortality of the Soul" (p. 8). It might be more accurate to say that Druidism is not a Christian religion but a pagan religion.

Applicants must be "of unblemished character, mentally and bodily sound." They must also "recognize and respect the Supreme Power of the Universe." Applicants must be between the ages of eighteen and fifty if they wish to participate in the lodge's insurance benefits. A hospitalization plan is open to members and their wives who have not reached the age of fifty-five.

Membership figures are not readily available but the *California Druid* magazine published in San Francisco has a circulation of 6000 copies.

Eagles
(Fraternal Order of Eagles)

Gradually the Fraternal Order of Eagles has been jettisoning the elements of secrecy which characterize most of the other organizations in this handbook. A publication of the F.O.E. observes: "In line with modern needs and up-to-date procedures, the colorful regalia trappings of yesterday are no longer. Gone, too, is the secret password, the roughhouse initiation."

When a group of theater owners in Seattle, Washington, got together in 1898 to form the fun organization which they called the "Seattle Order of Good Things" they laid the foundations for the Fraternal Order of Eagles. Chief founder John Cort and the other theatrical people in the first lodge met on the stage of a local theater to conduct the business of the Order. In a few years they adopted the eagle as their animal model and now, with the Elks and Moose, form the trio of animal lodges.

The lodge's early emphasis on conviviality and hedonism did not win everyone's favor. A writer in *McClure's* magazine in 1910 would describe the Eagles as "a great national organization of sporting men, bartenders, politicians, thieves, and professional criminals."

Almost seventy years after its founding the F.O.E. has broadened its original objective of providing a good time for its members to that of offering a social program for the Eagle, his wife, and children. An Eagle pamphlet explains: "The emphasis has shifted from solely recreation to a more balanced program of fun and fraternal activities of wide scope. The accent now is no longer on secrecy but rather service." The Aeries still sponsor drill teams and bands, conduct secret initiations, and observe lodge anniversaries.

The 850,000 Eagles need not apologize for the caliber of men who have joined their ranks. They include five presidents: Theodore Roosevelt, Warren Harding, Franklin D. Roosevelt, Harry S. Truman, and John F. Kennedy. Other well known Eagles are Chief Justice Earl Warren, J. Edgar Hoover, the late Father Flanagan of Boys Town, the late Senator Robert Wagner, Jack Dempsey, and Stan Musial. In 1948 the Eagles reported 1,000,000 members; this total dipped to 750,000 before starting to climb again.

More than any other fraternal organization the Eagles have promoted the adoption of advanced social legislation. The F.O.E. championed workmen's compensation, mothers' pensions, the eight-hour day, old age pensions, and the social security act. When President Roosevelt signed the social security act in 1935 he presented the pen to the Eagles for "their unselfish services." Currently the Order is urging enactment of "Jobs After 40" legislation which would ban job discrimination based on age; so far twenty-five states have enacted such laws.

Eagles have taken an interest in preserving their favorite bird from extinction. They have supported the National Audubon Society in its efforts to save the bald eagle and in 1963 backed federal legislation to extend protection to the golden eagles as well as the bald eagles.

At one time the Eagles lodge sold life insurance as a fraternal benefit society but it quit accepting new policyholders after 1927. Today a new member may become a beneficial or a nonbeneficial member; the beneficial member pays somewhat higher dues to receive sick and funeral benefits.

In 1941 the F.O.E. donated a dormitory to Boys Town in Omaha, Nebraska, and since then the Order has built Eagle Hall at Home on the Range for Boys in Sentinel Butte, North Dakota, and a dormitory at High Sky Girls Ranch near Midland, Texas. The Eagles' Memorial Foundation, started in 1946, provides financial aid for medical, dental, and educational expenses of children of Eagles who gave their lives as members of the armed forces. The Order has also made grants for research in cancer, muscular dystrophy, and heart disease.

Since World War II the Eagles have cooperated with CARE to equip youth training centers overseas. The first of these was set up in West Berlin in 1954. The Eagles persuaded the occupation authorities to turn over an old building. Here they have been training poor boys to become carpenters. Other Eagles houses have been started in Naples, Sicily, Manila, Mexico City, Chile, Iran, Greece, Turkey, Ecuador, Cebu, Tunisia, and Israel.

To be eligible for membership in the F.O.E. a man must belong to the Caucasian race, believe in a Supreme Being, possess a good moral character, and be over twenty-one. Communists are specifically excluded; chances are few apply.

During the initiation of a new member the president of the Aerie asks the candidate to repeat after him: "Before God, and on my honor, I promise that I will never make known to anyone the rituals of this Order, except to Eagles in good standing, and then only if I am authorized to do so." He also promises not to join an illegal organization of Eagles and to obey the laws of the Order, be loyal to his country, respect the sanctity of another Eagle's home, etc. He concludes: "I understand the meaning of these pledges and I ask my God and my Brothers to help me keep them. I acknowledge that the wilful violation of any of them is just cause for expulsion from the Order."

After a prayer by the chaplain, the "Ode to the Candidates," and instructions about the F.O.E. the new members are presented to the Aerie. The lodge also conducts a memorial service on or near Memorial Day and a final tribute to deceased Eagles if such a service is requested by the survivors.

Order of the Eastern Star

Since orthodox Freemasons have always refused to admit women into their lodges their female relatives have sometimes expressed dissatisfaction that they are excluded from the secret rites and mysteries of the Craft. To give the ladies a glimpse of Masonic arcana and perhaps to squelch feminine objections to lodge membership, an American Mason invented the Order of the Eastern Star.

This Order has proved to be one of the most successful of the dozens of Masonic satellites. In 1965 the OES enrolled more than 3,000,000 Master Masons and their wives, mothers, widows, sisters, and daughters in some 13,000 chapters.

So-called Adoptive Masonry or Masonry for women can be found on the continent as early as the eighteenth century. The Duchess of Bourbon was appointed Grand Mistress of Adoptive Masonry in France in 1775. She directed an order which worked four degrees: Apprentice, Companion, Mistress, and Perfect Mistress. Adoptive Masonry also gained some popularity in Holland, Italy, and Germany. The ladies did not receive the degrees of Freemasonry but degrees invented by the sponsors of Adoptive Masonry. These female lodges were "adopted" by regular Masonic lodges.

Although the Order of the Eastern Star can be considered the American version of Adoptive Masonry it forms no part of pure and ancient Freemasonry; the state grand lodges of Masons exercise no control over the OES. A Master Mason must, however, serve as patron of each Eastern Star chapter and he must be present at each initiation.

The Masonic encyclopedist Albert G. Mackey looked on the Eastern Star with some coolness and observed: "When a woman is informed that, by passing through the brief and unimpressive ceremony of any one of these degrees, she has become a Mason, the deception is still more gross and inexcusable" (*Encyclopedia of Freemasonry,* p. 38).

A Masonic enthusiast, Robert Morris, invented the Order of the Eastern Star which he first introduced as the American Adoptive Rite. He published a five-degree ritual in 1857 and revised it in 1865 under the title *The Rosary of the Eastern Star.* His original purpose seems to have been to devise signs of recognition by which women could reveal their Masonic connections to other Masons.

Morris was not much of an organizer and his new rite found few supporters among the leaders of American Freemasonry at that time. Growth was slow. In 1866 Morris turned over the rights to the rite to the Masonic publisher Robert Macoy, who also reworked the ritual.

The General Grand Chapter, largest of the three Eastern Star jurisdictions, was founded in Indianapolis in 1876. Within eight years of this founding the Order counted 50,000 women members and Master Masons.

Only women over eighteen who are related to Masons and who profess a belief in the existence of a Supreme Being may be initiated. The two chief officers of a subordinate chapter are the Worthy Matron and the Worthy Patron, a Master Mason. The duties of the chaplain of the chapter are to lead the chapter in its devotions at the altar and to invoke the blessings of the Heavenly Father upon their work. An open Bible rests on the altar in the center of the chapter room.

The five-degree ritual is based on the stories of five women of the Old and New Testaments: Adah the daughter, Ruth the widow, Esther the wife, Martha the sister, and Electa the mother. Eastern Star members may also be chosen to receive the complementary degree of Queen of the South.

Both men and woman may be initiated in the same ceremony. In the case of a woman the Associate Conductress removes the hat, gloves, and wrap of the candidate. She places a thin white veil over the head and face of the candidate and leads her to the door of the chapter room. Inside the Worthy Matron tells the candidate: "Your connection with the Masonic Order, and the recommendations which you bring, assure us that you are worthy to be entrusted with the light and knowledge of our Order.

One of the beneficent purposes of Freemasonry is to secure the welfare of the mothers, wives, sisters and daughters of Master Masons. The Order of the Eastern Star is designed to further this aim. The Masonic principles of Fraternal Love, Friendly Aid, and Truth are here declared and taught."

One of the landmarks of the OES states: "The Obligation of our Order, voluntarily assumed, is perpetual, from the force of which there is no release." The Worthy Patron, a Master Mason, administers the obligation while the candidate kneels at the altar holding an open Bible against her breast:

> I hereby pledge the sacred honor of a woman (or a Master Mason) to the faithful performance of the conditions of the following obligation: I will maintain with vigilance the absolute secrecy to which I now assent, promising never to reveal unlawfully any of the ceremonies, signs or passes of the Order of the Eastern Star.
>
> I will not be present nor assist in conferring these degrees on any man not Masonically known by me to be a Master Mason, nor any lady not vouched for by a Master Mason as being the wife, widow, sister, mother or daughter of a Master Mason.
>
> I will obey the constitution and laws and regulations of of the Grand Chapter, and the by-laws of the Subordinate Chapter of which I may be a member.
>
> I will relieve the necessities of a brother or sister of these degrees, (if they apply to me as such and are found worthy), as far as their necessities may require and my ability permit. Furthermore, I will not speak disrespectfully of a worthy brother or sister of these degrees, but will give them due and timely notice, that they may ward off approaching danger.
>
> In the presence of Almighty God, and before these witnesses, I do make this solemn pledge.

The conductress leads the candidate to the first point of the star and removes the veil from the candidate's face.

A member representing Adah relates the story of Jeph-thah's daughter. She explains the sign of this first degree which consists of raising and lowering the veil. The conductress leads the candidate to the next position where Ruth relates the history of Ruth, to Esther for the story of Esther, to Martha, and to Electa. Each instruction is considered a degree but the entire five-degree system is worked at one time.

At the conclusion of the five instructions the Worthy Matron gives another address which states in part:

> We are not a part of the Masonic institution, yet we are connected with Masonry by intimate and tender ties . . . To us are given all the advantages of the society, its shield of protection, its hand of relief, and its voice of sympathy. The only Masonic privilege denied to us is that of visiting the lodge. Women cannot be made Masons. This is a rule that has been handed down with other rules of Masonry for thousands of years. Each Mason present pledged himself before he was admitted into the lodge that he would never allow any of the ancient rules of Masonry to be changed, and this is one of them. Therefore, Masons cannot invite us to visit their lodges. But as I have said, they can, and do, and will share with us in all the solid privileges and benefits of Masonry, and thus practically unite us with them in this great, this glorious, this heavenly work of doing good.

Jewish and other non-Christian relatives of Masons are not barred from the Order of the Eastern Star but certain elements of the ritual might make such initiates feel uncomfortable. At one point, for example, the Worthy Patron explains that "Henceforth you will be known as one of the members of this Order whose inspiration is the Star of Bethlehem, directing all the faithful to that city not made with hands, the New Jerusalem." The general motto of the OES is "We have seen His star in the East, and are come to worship Him."

The sign for the fifth degree is made by crossing the arms over the breast while casting the eyes upward; the explanation is that this sign represents "Electa clasping the crucifix to her bosom, depicting her love for the Saviour." The degree of Martha is intended to demonstrate faith in the Redeemer and describes the events surrounding the raising of her brother Lazarus from the dead by Jesus. Electa is identified as "the elect lady" in St. John's second epistle.

The General Grand Chapter governs Eastern Star chapters in all but two of the states of the union and in Mexico, Cuba, the Philippines, the Netherlands, West Indies, Japan, and Germany. The Independent Grand Chapter of New York and New Jersey governs chapters in those two states.

The Supreme Grand Chapter of Scotland has jurisdiction over the Order in Scotland, England, South Africa, South Wales, Australia, and New Zealand. The Grand Lodge of England thoroughly disapproves of the Eastern Star and threatens with expulsion any English Mason who receives its degrees or consents to serve as Worthy Patron.

In the United States the Order of the Eastern Star maintains seventeen homes, hospitals, and orphanages. Its headquarters is in Washington, D. C. Members of the Order encourage girls to join Job's Daughters and the Rainbow Girls. In many ways the Eastern Star cooperates with Freemasonry and often uses Masonic lodges as meeting places.

The Roman Catholic Church bans membership in the Eastern Star since this Order constitutes an auxiliary of the Masonic fraternity. The same penalty of excommunication would apply to a Catholic woman who joined the Eastern Star as to a man who took the Masonic oaths. The various Protestant churches which oppose secret societies put the Eastern Star into the condemned category.

(See **Amaranth, Order of,** and **White Shrine of Jerusalem**)

Elks

(Benevolent and Protective Order of Elks of the United States of America)

Had the New York state legislature not passed a law in 1866 closing the saloons on Sunday, the nation probably would not have seen the birth of the Benevolent and Protective Order of Elks. Many booze-loving citizens, including a group of actors in New York City, looked for ways to sidestep the new Sabbath law. The actors rented a room first on Fourteenth Street and later on the Bowery where they could refresh their spirits after a week behind the footlights.

Gradually this group of sociable thespians gave a more formal structure to their Sunday evening drinking society. They called themselves the "Jolly Corks." Whether they took this name from the corks which popped from their bottles of whiskey and gin or from the burnt cork which they used as theatrical makeup is debatable. A cork played a part in their initiation of new members and each Jolly Cork had to carry a cork on his person or pay for a round of drinks. Their leader was an English actor, the son of an Anglican parson, Charles Algernon S. Vivian.

The need for a more dignified name was recognized as the Jolly Corks started to initiate members from outside the theatrical and literary professions. Some of the Jolly Corks observed an elk's head on exhibit at P. T. Barnum's museum and decided to rename their growing society after this impressive beast. A current publication of the lodge explains:

> The animal from which the Order took its name was chosen because a number of its attributes were deemed typical of those to be cultivated by members of the fraternity. The elk is distinctively an American animal. It habitually lives in herds. The largest of our native quadrupeds, it is yet

fleet of foot and graceful in movement. It is quick and keen of perception; and while it is usually gentle and even timorous, it is strong and valiant in defense of its own. (*What It Means to Be an Elk,* p. 7.)

The Order considers February 16, 1868, to be its date of founding. It states its own purposes as the practice of the four cardinal virtues of charity, justice, brotherly love, and fidelity; the promotion of the welfare and happiness of its members; the fostering of patriotism; and the cultivation of good fellowship.

Then as now the Masonic influence on the BPOE was evident in many ways. Stevens comments:

. . . those who so shaped its destinies as to make it one of the leading brotherhoods among the few not founded on political or financial considerations, may be safely classed as Freemasons; for the ceremonial of the Elks, although it has been changed several times, still presents features familiar to workmen from the quarries (*Cyclopaedia of Fraternities,* p. 230).

Some evidence of the Masonic heritage of the BPOE can be seen in the use of aprons as lodge regalia, the use of the distinctively Masonic term "tyler" to designate the guardian of the lodge room, the "Lodge of Sorrow" for a deceased Elk. Unlike the Masonic lodges in the United States the Elks lodges allow the sale of liquor in their clubs and offer toasts of alcoholic beverages.

Membership in the BPOE is limited to "white male citizens of the United States, not under twenty-one years of age, who believe in the existence of God." Furthermore no one will be admitted "who is directly or indirectly a member of or in any way connected or affiliated with the Communist Party, or who believes in the overthrow of our Government by force." The racial exclusiveness of the Elks exceeds even that of the United States Masonic lodges which refuse to initiate Negroes but will accept candidates who are American Indians or people of oriental background.

The BPOE is organized into a grand lodge and subordinate lodges. The latter may be established only in United States cities which have "within their respective corporate limits not less than five thousand white inhabitants." A city may have one Elks lodge for every 500,000 population or major fraction thereof. Thus a city of as many as 700,000 people might have dozens of Masonic lodges but only one Elks lodge with perhaps thousands of members.

What It Means to Be an Elk states: "The Order questions no man's religion; nor bars him on account of his creed. It is not concerned with one's political affiliations. And it does not permit either religion or politics to be injected into, or have any effect upon, its fraternal deliberations, national or local" (p. 5).

The patriotic not to say nationalistic orientation of the BPOE is demonstrated by its refusal to initiate anyone who is not a United States citizen, the promotion of Flag Day on June 14 as a major lodge activity, the place of honor of the American flag on the lodge altar, and the pledge of allegiance to the flag which closes each lodge meeting. The Elks have engaged in widespread war relief in World Wars I and II and have always remembered the patients in veterans' hospitals.

In opening an Elks lodge the esquire goes to the station of the esteemed loyal knight, picks up the Bible and places it upon the altar. The organist plays *Nearer, My God, to Thee*. The esquire declares: "This is the Bible, the Book of the Law, upon which is founded Justice." The members now sing:

> Great Ruler of the Universe
>   All-seeing and benign
> Look down upon and bless our work,
>   And be all glory Thine;

E

> May charity as taught us here
> Be ever borne in mind
> The Golden Rule our motto true,
> For days of Auld Lang Syne.

Auld Lang Syne has become the recognized fraternal anthem of the BPOE. No prayers offered in an Elks lodge include the name of Christ since not all Elks are Christians. Each Elks lodge appoints a chaplain who offers prayer in the name of the members.

The Elks lodge works only one degree. *What It Means to Be an Elk* states that the initiation "is conducted throughout with dignity and decorum. It is wholly devoid of any feature which will embarrass or annoy the candidate, or subject him to ridicule or to any discomfort, physical or mental."

In an initiation the exalted ruler explains that a candidate must "take the solemn and binding oath and obligation of the Benevolent and Protective Order of Elks." The candidate is assured that "there is nothing which will . . . conflict with your religious or political opinions." The candidate affirms his belief in God and is then instructed to lift up his right hand above the altar and to hold his left hand over his heart. The chaplain offers a prayer before the exalted ruler begins the oath which the prospective Elk repeats. It is lengthy and bears many similarities to the Masonic oaths. The oath begins:

> I, ..., in the presence of God and this lodge of Elks, do solemnly promise and swear that I will never reveal any of the confidential matters of this Order which have been or may hereafter be, committed to my charge and keeping.

The candidate goes on to swear to obey the constitution and rules of the BPOE, to uphold the Constitution of the United States, to propose no unworthy purpose for membership, to cast ballots for the good of the Order, to obey all lawful summonses, never to reveal the names of those receiving help from the lodge, not to use the membership for business purposes, never to introduce politics or religion in lodge meetings, to protect a fellow Elk, etc.

He concludes:

> If I break this oath, may I wander through the world forsaken; may I be pointed out as a being bereft of decency and manhood, unfit to hold communion with true and upright men. And may God help me, and keep me steadfast in this my solemn and binding obligation in the Benevolent and Protective Order of Elks of the United States of America. Amen.

Both the Masonic and Elks oaths would seem to qualify as solemn oaths which the Church considers acts of religion. The only difference is that the Elks oath does not entail the penalties of suicide and self-mutilation attached to the Masonic oaths.

Each Elks lodge conducts other services with set rituals and religious significance. The first Sunday in December is known as Elks Memorial Day and the second Sunday in May is Mother's Day. Whenever an Elks lodge is in session at 11 p.m. the brothers participate in the "Eleven O'Clock Toast" to absent brothers; the toast may be made on other fraternal occasions or even when small groups of Elks meet together at this hour. The lodge may be asked to conduct a funeral service to supplant or supplement a religious funeral. This is known as a "Lodge of Sorrow." The assembled Elks are assured that their departed brother has "passed into the light which is beyond the valley of the shadow of death." There is also a ritual at the graveside.

The national lodge prescribes rituals for the dedication of an Elks building, the consecration of an Elks cemetery or burial plot, the laying of a cornerstone, and other occasions.

For many decades the Catholic Church discouraged the faithful from joining an Elks lodge. The solemn oaths, the Masonic background of the lodge, its religious features were enough to brand the BPOE as inappropriate for Catholics. In 1924, for example, Preuss was able to write in his standard *Dictionary of Secret and Other Societies:* "The better part of the Catholic press has long since agreed that the Elks are no fit society for Catholics to belong to" (p. 62).

The Catholic Church, however, never took an official stand against the BPOE and many Catholics including well-known laymen such as Alfred E. Smith and James A. Farley wore the Elks apron. Today thousands of Roman Catholics swear the Elks oaths and find no difficulty reconciling membership in the Elks and the Church. The Church leaves the question of swearing the Elks oaths to the conscience of the individual Catholic. Certain Protestant denominations such as the Lutheran Church-Missouri Synod, Wisconsin Synod, and Christian Reformed Church classify the Elks with Freemasonry as a forbidden society. An evaluation by the Commission on Fraternal Organizations of the Lutheran Church-Missouri Synod concludes:

The Order has all the earmarks of a fraternal organization with objectionable religious features even though there is less emphasis on the religious than in Freemasonry. The provisions in the ritual for chaplain, prayer, Bible, altar, religious songs and sentiments betray the importance of the religious element. At the same time these features bear the marks of a non-Christian piety and religiosity. The Order exemplifies a religious access to God outside of Jesus Christ.

Each of the 2000 lodges may choose its own projects of community betterment and charity; the national headquarters of the BPOE estimates that the lodges contribute about $8,000,000 a year for these purposes. There are also a number of projects supported by the entire Order. They include the Elks National Home in the foothills of the Blue Ridge mountains near Bedford, Virginia. The aged and indigent Elks who live at the home enjoy private rooms.

The Order appropriates about $500,000 a year for the benefit of hospitalized veterans of the armed forces. It contributes $400,000 a year for college scholarships, grants for the advanced training of technicians in cerebral palsy therapy, and other charitable endeavors. Only the income is used from the $8,000,000 Elks National Foundation; since its founding in 1928 this foundation has provided more than $3,000,000 for humanitarian purposes.

No auxiliaries or affiliated groups are recognized by the BPOE. However, female relatives of Elks form the membership of the Benevolent and Protective Order of Does and of the Emblem Club. Young men may join Antlers clubs sponsored by local Elks.

A few Elks lodges are said to permit business or social affiliations without obligating these members to participate in the ritual or to swear the oaths. The Grand Lodge disallows such procedures and insists that the only legitimate Elks are those who are properly and fully initiated.

Barred from membership in the BPOE, Negroes founded the Improved Benevolent and Protective Order of Elks. A railroad porter, Arthur J. Riggs, organized the first lodge of Negro Elks in 1898 in Cincinnati. He compiled a ritual similar to that used in the BPOE and obtained a copyright. In 1906 the white Elks succeeded in persuading the New York state legislature to pass a law forbidding a Negro from calling himself an Elk or wearing an Elk emblem; the law has no force today. The Improved BPOE has become one of the largest and most influential Negro lodges; it claims more than 300,000 members.

Foresters

Just as the Freemasons employ the tools and terminology of the building trade to inculcate fraternal lessons so the Foresters employ the appurtenances of the woodsman. One of the oldest fraternal systems and still one of the largest in England, the Order of Foresters has suffered a number of schisms.

Besides the Catholic Order of Foresters which was discussed earlier (p. 15), the two major branches in North America are the Ancient Order of Foresters and the Independent Order of Foresters. Both of these lodges maintain headquarters in Toronto, Canada. There are several smaller groups of Foresters.

Although the Ancient Order of Foresters claims to go back to 1798, the first historical record of the lodge is dated 1813. For its secret ritual the Foresters drew on the legends of Robin Hood, Friar Tuck, Little John, and the Merrie Men.

The Ancient Order admits men and women between sixteen and fifty who are "of good moral character, sound in health, and free from disease." It is primarily a sick and death benefit society.

A schism in 1874 resulted in formation of the Independent Order of Foresters. It reports 366,269 members in 545 lodges presided over by Chief Rangers. This Order makes a special effort to care for members afflicted with tuberculosis, cancer, or polio.

(See **Catholic Order of Foresters**)

Fraternal Order of Police

While the criminal elite may belong to the Mafia the policemen of the nation may join their own secret organization: the Fraternal Order of Police. Any full-time policeman — patrolman to chief, man or woman — who works for a municipal, state, or federal government may join the FOP. Currently about 57,000 policemen belong to 577 lodges in thirty-five states. The FOP is the only national police organization.

In a way the FOP serves as a labor union for policemen although the lodge forbids any strikes and relies on persuasion to achieve better working conditions, pay, and pension plans for its members.

This occupational lodge was formed in 1915 in Pittsburgh at a time when many communities expected policemen to work twelve-hour days, seven days a week at low pay. Unlike labor unions which bar supervisory personnel the FOP has always enlisted police chiefs as well as detectives, lieutenants, and patrolmen.

At least ten policemen are needed to form a subordinate lodge. Most of these lodges provide a death benefit and a sick benefit in cities where no sick leave is authorized by the police department. Each local lodge is autonomous. Three or more subordinate lodges form the eighteen state lodges and delegates from all of the subordinate lodges meet biennially in the Grand Lodge. National headquarters is in Cincinnati.

A chaplain opens and closes lodge meetings with prayer but the Fraternal Order of Police lodge room does not include an altar or open Bible. Candidates for admission repeat the following obligation:

I, ..., in the presence of the Creator of the Universe and the members of the Fraternal Order of Police here assembled, do most solemnly and sincerely promise and swear, that I will to the best of my ability comply with all the laws and rules of this Order; that I will recognize the authority of my legally elected officers and obey all orders

F

therefrom not in conflict with my religious or political views, or my right as an American citizen; that I will not cheat, wrong, or defraud this Order, or any member thereof, or permit the same to be done if in my power to prevent it; that I will at all times aid and assist a worthy Brother in sickness or distress, so far as it lies in my power to do so; that I will not divulge any of the secrets of this Order to any one not entitled to receive them. To all of which I most solemnly and sincerely promise and swear. Should I violate this, my solemn obligation, I hereby consent to be expelled from the Order.

The FOP displays most of the other features of the typical lodge. To gain admission to the lodge room the member must give the password to the guard at the door. Once inside the member advances to the chair and gives the countersign. The vice-president of the lodge receives a military salute. The sign of recognition is made by grasping the lobe of the left ear between the thumb and finger of the left hand. There is also a sign of distress and a secret grip.

The Grand Lodge publishes an annual survey of salaries and working conditions for policemen in 1400 cities and towns. Local lodges promote safety programs and youth work. Some sponsor ladies auxiliaries.

Fraternities, College

Millions of American men and women received their first taste of the ritual, oaths, and other apparatus of the secret society when they joined a college fraternity or sorority. On some campuses the majority of students belong to Greek-letter social fraternities while on some other campuses such secret organizations are strictly forbidden.

Here we are speaking about social fraternities. Two

other types which also use Greek letters in their names are the professional and the honorary fraternities. These are associations which band together students and graduates in particular professions or which recognize scholastic achievement.

Membership in a social fraternity is usually limited to sophomores, juniors, and seniors. Many colleges expect freshmen to live in residence halls. The contest for members is known as "rushing" and it is during this rush period that the prospective members are entertained at smokers (or teas) and scrutinized by the active members. Those who are invited to join become pledges and after a trial period they undergo a secret initiation. In most cases social fraternities and sororities maintain chapter houses where the actives and pledges live, eat, sleep, and study.

All social fraternities forbid membership in more than one such fraternity although a member may also join a professional or honorary fraternity. By custom, if not constitution, most white fraternities exclude Negroes and some also refuse to pledge Jewish students. On the other hand, some fraternities have been organized specifically for Jews, Negroes, Roman Catholics, Masons, and Lutherans.

Each fraternity develops its own traditions. One common custom is the bestowal of the fraternity pin on a young lady which indicates that the couple is going steady and probably headed for engagement. Rivalry is common between the Greeks and the independents who are students who remain outside of the fraternity-sorority system and live instead in residence halls, private homes, or co-op houses.

Property owned by fraternities and sororities is assessed in the hundreds of millions of dollars. Some chapter houses for fifty or sixty members can only be described as mansions. Fraternity bureaucrats preside over the national headquarters and supervise the affairs of the organization which includes publication of a magazine, songbook, directory, etc. Sixty-one fraternities belong to the National Interfraternity Council, organized in 1909, and thirty sororities belong to the National Panhellenic Conference, 1902. In addition there are dozens of local or weaker Greek-letter organizations on American college campuses.

After graduation the fraternity or sorority member may continue his affiliation as an alumni member which usually involves payment of annual dues. He may also expect more or less regular appeals for funds for national projects or building programs. Control of most of the major fraternities rests with alumni who graduated twenty-five or thirty years ago and who often attempt to impose the campus mores of their own college days.

Critics of the Greek system concentrate on its racial exclusiveness, social snobbery, drinking habits, and the hazards of initiation pranks. Professor Alfred McClung Lee has denounced the relative lack of supervision in many chapter houses. "A fraternity house thus frequently has the spirit of a household from which the parents are temporarily absent, where the children and their friends have taken over" (*Fraternities Without Brotherhood*, p. 27). Counselors have decried the traumatic experience of eighteen- and nineteen-year-old coeds who are rejected by the sorority of their choice during the rush period.

The Greeks themselves defend their fraternities by appealing to the right of private association which allows them to bar any who do not meet the racial or religious qualifications for membership. They insist that the acquisition of social poise, opportunities for leadership, social activities, alumni contacts, and experience in group living more than compensate for any disadvantages.

Phi Beta Kappa was the first social fraternity organized in this country. When it was founded at the College of William and Mary in 1776 it included all the ingredients — ritual, oath, signs, badge, and motto — which identify a social fraternity today. Chapters were set up at Harvard and Yale in 1779. Not long after its founding Phi Beta Kappa turned into the scholastic honorary fraternity which is well known today.

The first social fraternity to retain its social character was Kappa Alpha, founded at Union College in 1826. It was followed in 1827 by Sigma Phi and Delta Phi at the same college. The first sorority was Kappa Alpha Theta, founded at De Pauw in 1870. An older women's organization known as I. C. Sorosis was started at Monmouth College in 1867 and changed its name to Pi Beta Phi in 1870.

The anti-Masonic agitation from 1827 to 1840 hampered the growth of the earlier campus secret societies and brought some condemnations by church leaders but by the end of the Civil War the Greek system had won recognition on scores of campuses. Only one national social fraternity remains nonsecret; Delta Upsilon was founded at Williams College as a protest against the secrecy of fraternities.

Most Greek initiations have been frankly modeled after the Masonic ritual. Stevens observed:

> . . . some of the better known college fraternities give unmistakable evidence, to those of their members in a position to judge, of having rummaged in the bureau drawers of Freemasonry, Odd Fellowship, Forestry, the Templars, Knights of Malta, and other "orders" for ritualistic finery. Zeta Psi was founded by Freemasons. Delta Psi, Columbia, 1847, was dressed up by someone who had access to the rituals of the bastard Masonic rites of Misraim and Memphis. Psi Upsilon hung its harp low on the tree of symbolic Masonry (*Cyclopaedia of Fraternities,* p. 346).

William H. Shideler, founder of Phi Kappa Tau and a Mason himself, observed: "Most of the rituals of college fraternities are based more or less directly upon the old

Morgan exposé of the Masonic ritual. In many cases even the phraseology of the obligation is preserved in greater or less detail."

During the initiation the pledges swear to keep secret the mysteries of the rites and to refuse to join any other social fraternity. Equipment manufacturers for fraternities and sororities advertise robes, Bibles, altars, candlesticks, crowns, staffs, censers, and incense as necessary paraphernalia for secret initiations.

For years the formal initiation was preceded by a week of pranks and hazing known as Hell Week. During these days the active members made life miserable for the pledges in innumerable ingenious ways. Not every prank ended in hilarity. Many young men have died during these fraternity hazings from poison, suffocation, burns, accidents. Recently the more responsible fraternities have turned Hell Week into Help Week during which the members undertake worthwhile community projects such as painting a local church, cleaning a neglected river bank, helping a poor family. A Greek spokesman comments, "The change of Hell Week, the most destructive feature ever adopted by fraternities, into Help Week, has done more to create good will than anything else in the history of the Greeks" (*Baird's Manual of American College Fraternities,* 16 ed., p. 37).

Some colleges and universities have encouraged the growth of the fraternity and sorority systems since the building of chapter houses for student-members relieved the institutions of the need to provide residence facilities. Where housemothers were employed by the chapters the school did not have to provide its own counselors. Many college administrators belonged to Greek organizations in their own undergraduate days and strongly believe in the values of the Greek way of life. Yet some of the most prominent institutions in the country ban all social fraternities: Princeton, Notre Dame, West Point, Fordham, the

Citadel, Smith, Georgetown, California Institute of Technology, Annapolis, Radcliffe, Bryn Mawr, Oberlin, Haverford, Virginia Military Institute, and Wooster.

In recent years the fraternities and sororities have come under heavy attack from civil rights proponents and liberals because of their "white only" policies. Some universities such as the University of Colorado, the University of Connecticut, and the State University of New York have issued ultimatums to Greek-letter organizations to remove racial restrictions from their constitutions and bylaws or leave the campus.

Barred from the all-white fraternities, Negro college students started to form their own Greek organizations in 1906. The four major Negro fraternities and four sororities will admit white pledges but remain predominantly Negro in membership.

The list of well-known Americans who have belonged to college fraternities and sororities would take many pages. A fraternity booklet maintains that, with only two exceptions in each office, every president and vice-president of the United States born since 1825 has been a fraternity man.

Greek-letter societies are active on 497 campuses where they enroll about 250,000 men and 100,000 women. The total number of men and women affiliated with these societies as pledges, actives, and alumni members is about 2,265,000.

Although many college students still pledge Greek organizations, the percentage of Greeks on United States campuses has declined drastically since World War II. Veterans turned their backs on the horseplay and extra costs of fraternity life and seldom joined a fraternity. Recently the tremendous growth of student bodies has forced colleges and universities to erect more and more residence halls, some of which can accommodate more men than can a dozen fraternity houses. Across the nation the percentage of college students in fraternities and sororities has declined from 30 percent before the war to about 15 percent. Nevertheless the investment in chapter houses, the support of alumni members, and the desire of many for this type of living experience will probably insure the survival of the Greek system for many decades.

(See **Acacia**)

Freemasonry

For nearly 250 years men have knelt to swear the solemn oaths of the Masonic lodges. Freemasonry was organized in England but four out of five of the world's Freemasons now live in the United States. They and their brothers in other countries have made Freemasonry the largest international secret society.

The Masonic lodge has also furnished the model for most of the hundreds of secret societies founded in Western nations during the eighteenth and nineteenth centuries. Some men who belonged to a lower social class than that which populated the Masonic lodges formed other secret fraternities such as the Odd Fellows; some who avoided Masonry for religious reasons appropriated elements of the Masonic apparatus when they established societies such as the Knights of Columbus.

Legendary Masonry goes back to the building of King Solomon's temple when Hiram Abiff, a mason, is said to have chosen death rather than reveal the secret masonic word. No serious historian attaches any credence to this legend. The beginnings of modern Freemasonry can be found in the crafts or guilds of working masons in medieval times. These masons adopted a system of signs and passwords which served the purpose of a "union card." Their worksheds were known as lodges.

When the building of cathedrals declined after the Protestant Reformation, membership in the masons' lodges fell. Some lodges began to admit honorary and nonworking members to bolster their membership rolls. Eventually these nonworking members outnumbered the working members and the character of the lodges changed. The secrets of Masonry, such as the passwords, symbols, and grips, were employed to inculcate certain moral and religious lessons.

Four of the surviving lodges met on June 24, 1717, and formed the Grand Lodge of England, the mother lodge. Dr. James Anderson (1684–1739), a Scottish Presbyterian minister, wrote the Book of Constitutions published in 1723 and revised in 1738. His Constitutions remains the basic charter of speculative Freemasonry although the Craft has changed its character from a philosophical to a quasi-religious nature in Anglo-Saxon countries.

During the medieval period the operative masons were advised to remain loyal to the Catholic Church; the speculative Freemasons in England were invited to follow "that Religion to which all men agree, leaving their particular opinions to themselves." Originally English Freemasonry was deistic; the lodges applied a distinctly deistic name to God: the Great Architect of the Universe.

No one has the power to change the "landmarks" or essential features of Freemasonry; various Masonic authorities have proposed between fifteen and twenty-five such landmarks. Most United States authorities agree that the landmarks include the three-degree system including the Royal Arch, the Hiramic legend of the third degree, the methods of recognition, belief in the Great Architect of the Universe and in the immortality of the soul, the place of the Volume of Sacred Law on the altar, the equality of all Masons in the lodge, the necessity of secrecy, the right of a Mason to visit every regular lodge in the world, and the symbolical method of teaching. At least Anglo-Saxon lodges consider these as basic features of authentic Freemasonry; when the Grand Orient of France in 1877 removed the Bible from its altars and no longer demanded belief in the GAOTU the Anglo-Saxon lodges severed fraternal relations with the Grand Orient. This schism persists to this day.

No religious test is administered by Masonic lodges so long as the applicant expresses a belief in some power higher than man. (The sole exception is the refusal of the Grand Lodge of Utah to admit any member of the Mormon Church.) Anderson's Constitutions states that a Mason "if he rightly understands the Art, will never be a stupid Atheist or an irreligious Libertine." Some scholars interpret this to mean that an intelligent atheist might well be welcomed in a lodge. At any rate Masonry will initiate a Christian, Jew, Moslem, Hindu, Parsee, Buddhist, or the adherent of any other religion. Those who prefer not to swear on the Christian Bible may choose another volume of Sacred Law such as the Koran, Vedas, or Pentateuch.

Until 1721 the Grand Lodge of England attracted few members but thereafter some members of royal society were initiated and lent considerable prestige to the Craft. Some men joined because they wearied of the interminable religious disputations of the age and yearned for a society based on the principles of naturalism. But before long Freemasonry took on the coloring of Protestant Christianity and has ever since won support from major segments of the Anglican establishment.

Irish Masons formed a rival grand lodge in England in 1751 and attracted large numbers of adherents. They were known as "Antients" or "York" Masons. A union of the two grand lodges was effected in 1813; the new United Grand

Lodge of England incorporated some of the pet features of the Antients, such as the Royal Arch degree.

Although ostracized from many areas of English life Roman Catholics were regularly initiated into the Masonic lodges. The lay leader of the Catholic community in England, Robert Edward, the ninth Lord Petre, became Grand Master of the English Grand Lodge in 1772 and remained in that office for five years. Another Grand Master, the Marquess of Ripon, resigned his office in 1874 when he joined the Catholic Church. In Ireland many Roman Catholics joined the lodges since the papal condemnation was not promulgated there for many decades. Daniel O'Connell was initiated in 1799 and served as Worshipful Master of Lodge Number 189 in Dublin. When the Church's attitude toward the Craft was made clear O'Connell renounced Freemasonry.

The total Masonic membership in England is given at 550,000 with another 400,000 in Scotland and 50,000 in Ireland. There are about 260,000 Masons in Canada and 440,000 in Australia and New Zealand.

From England Freemasonry spread to the continent. From their beginning in 1721 the French Masonic lodges attracted anticlericals as well as occultists.

The three German Christian lodges usually refused to initiate Jews; in 1935 the 77,000 German Masons gave their allegiance to eight rival grand lodges. Hitler declared war on Freemasonry, closing the lodges, destroying the ritual paraphernalia, and sometimes putting the members into concentration camps.

The kings of Scandinavian countries have traditionally served as Grand Masters and patrons of their grand lodges. Their rites are tinged with Christian elements which would be rejected by other Masons.

Generalissimo Franco closed all the Masonic lodges in Spain after the Civil War in which the Masons gave their support to the Loyalist cause. The lodges in Spain, Italy, Belgium, and Portugal have historically opposed the Catholic Church to a degree unknown in English and American Freemasonry.

The Grand Orients of Latin American countries have also expressed their hostility to Catholicism in many ways. They typically attempt to exclude the Church from any role in education or social action. In recent years the prestige and influence of Masonry has suffered a sharp decline in most Latin American nations. Until recently the largest Masonic constituency was reported by the Cuban Grand Lodge. Fidel Castro took over some of the lodge buildings while many of the leaders of Cuban Masonry fled to the United States. In Mexico twenty grand lodges claim Masonic jurisdiction and most of these receive no recognition from United States grand lodges.

Small Masonic bodies have been established in Greece, Japan, India, the Philippines, Formosa, Hong Kong, and the Netherlands.

The first civil governments to ban the Masonic lodges were those of Protestant states. Holland banned the lodge in 1735, Sweden and Geneva in 1738, Zurich in 1740, and Berne in 1745. Of course, these prohibitions are no longer enforced.

Soviet Russia banned Freemasonry in 1922; except as a possible underground movement Freemasonry no longer exists in the USSR, Red China, or the other Communist nations. Spain and Portugal do not recognize the legal existence of the lodge. President Sukarno has forbidden Masonic activities in Indonesia as has Nasser of the United Arab Republic.

In European countries Freemasonry has remained an elite movement. Masons on the continent seldom wear Masonic rings or lapel pins. They do not advertize their meetings. These Masons carefully select the men they invite to membership and expect all Masons to study the principles of Masonry and show an active interest in the lodge. They do not tolerate "fun" organizations such as the Shrine or Grotto.

It takes years for a continental Mason to advance from the 1st to the 32nd degree. He spends two years achieving the Master Mason degree and must then wait four years before he gets the 4th degree of the Scottish rite. From then on he takes about two degrees a year until he reaches the 32nd degree. In contrast the American Mason can become a Master Mason in a few weeks and can jump from 3rd to 32nd degree over a single weekend. American Freemasonry has become a mass movement with a consequent dilution of Masonic quality. In many towns of the Middle West and South almost every white Protestant gentleman belongs to a Masonic lodge.

Not many years after its founding in London the Craft crossed the Atlantic. Daniel Coxe was granted a deputation appointing him Provincial Grand Master of New York, New Jersey, and Pennsylvania in 1730. Benjamin Franklin joined one of the first American lodges and published an edition of Anderson's Constitutions in 1734. Both Antients and Moderns chartered lodges in the colonies.

During the American Revolution the lodges sometimes served as meeting places for the revolutionists. George Washington joined Fredericksburg Lodge Number 4 in Virginia in 1752. Some Freemasons supported independence and others fought for the king. Eight of the fifty-six signers of the Declaration of Independence are known to have been members of the lodge. Patrick Henry, Paul Revere, and John Paul Jones wore the apron of Masonry and so did Benedict Arnold.

During the latter part of the eighteenth century the papal prohibition against Freemasonry was not enforced by the Church in the colonies. Lord Baltimore became a Mason in

England in 1730 but did not promote the lodge in Maryland. Bishop John Carroll's brother, Daniel, was an enthusiastic Catholic and Mason. James Hoban, another Catholic Freemason, designed the capitol of the United States and was chief founder of Federal Lodge Number 1 in the District of Columbia.

American Freemasonry as well as all secret societies suffered a setback when Masons were accused of abducting and murdering Captain William Morgan of Batavia, New York, in 1826. Morgan had planned to publish an exposé of the Masonic rites. Preachers took to their pulpits and journalists to their pens to denounce the lodge as subversive and anti-Christian. Thousands of Masons burned their aprons and few men asked to join the lodge. Anti-Masons even formed a political party which nominated William Wirt for president in 1832 but carried only one state, Vermont. By 1840 the anti-Masonic agitation had died down and growth of the secret societies continued during the rest of the nineteenth century.

Twelve American presidents have been Freemasons: Washington, Jackson, Monroe, Polk, Andrew Johnson, Garfield, McKinley, Theodore Roosevelt, Taft, Harding, Franklin D. Roosevelt, and Truman. Harding received only the 1st degree in his hometown lodge but when he was elected president he quickly advanced from 1st to 32nd degree. Truman, the last Masonic president, once served as Grand Master of the Grand Lodge of Missouri. Eisenhower, and, of course, Kennedy, did not join the lodge; Johnson took the 1st degree in a lodge in Texas but did not continue and so would not be considered a Mason in good standing.

Some of the distinguished Americans who have been members of the Masonic lodge include John Jacob Astor, Irving Berlin, Luther Burbank, Henry Clay, Thomas E. Dewey, Henry Ford, Barry Goldwater, Samuel Gompers,

J. Edgar Hoover, Charles Lindbergh, General Douglas MacArthur, Andrew Mellon, General John J. Pershing, Will Rogers, Sigmund Romberg, John Philip Sousa, Mark Twain, and Chief Justice Earl Warren. In any single year the majority of state governors, United States senators, and United States representatives are likely to be Freemasons.

The 16,000 Blue or Symbolic Lodges enroll approximately 4,200,000 Masons in the United States while the Prince Hall lodges of Negro Masons claim another 312,000 men. There is no single grand lodge for this country; instead there are separate and independent grand lodges for each of the states, the District of Columbia, and Puerto Rico. The Masonic Service Association coordinates some lodge activities but has no power over the grand lodges.

Thirty-one of the state grand lodges maintain homes for children and old folks. Unlike, say, the Knights of Columbus or Foresters, the Masonic lodge does not provide insurance benefits for its members. Individual lodges may choose to establish sick and death benefit funds but these are likely to be small. Traditionally Masonic aid is extended only to Master Masons in good standing and their widows and orphans. As Coil explains: "In recent times, the Fraternity has been forced to realize that the Masonic duty of aid, assistance, and relief is due Masons only and, for practical reasons cannot be extended to outsiders" (*Coil's Masonic Encyclopedia,* p. 23). He points out that monthly dues of two or three dollars will not provide sufficient funds for the lodge to extend aid to outsiders. Of course, organizations with Masonic membership requirements such as the Shrine do offer assistance to non-Masons.

To a far greater degree than the English or continental Masons the Americans patronize the so-called higher degrees. The three basic Masonic degrees are those of Entered Apprentice, Fellow Craft, and Master Mason. In order to remain a member of any appended degree or fun organization the man must keep up membership in his Blue Lodge. This does not involve any attendance requirement but only regular payment of dues.

Master Masons may join fun organizations such as the Grotto and Tall Cedars of Lebanon. Along with their female relatives they may enter the Order of the Eastern Star. Some join the High Twelve luncheon club or Square and Compass clubs. Retired and active officers of the armed forces may belong to the National Sojourners. Deaf Masons find fellowship in the Desoms. The relatively few interested in Masonic philosophy have organized the Philalethes.

A Master Mason may elect to climb one or both of the two Masonic ladders of the higher rites: the Scottish or York rites. About 1,000,000 or one out of four Master Masons have taken the Scottish route. This rite, organized in the United States in 1801, consists of thirty-two degrees plus the honorary 33rd degree; however, the first three degrees are worked by the Blue or Symbolic Craft Lodge. Applicants to the Scottish rite pay a fee of about $150 and usually spend two or three days witnessing the enactment of the degrees in a Scottish rite cathedral. The rite seldom works all twenty-nine degrees because of the time it would involve; many of the degrees are simply summarized for the edification of the candidates. These "communicated" degrees consist of a short lecture and recitation of the oath of the degree. It is also possible for a candidate to take the degrees in stages rather than all at once.

Four subordinate bodies within the Scottish rite confer the degrees. In the Northern jurisdiction the Lodge of Perfection confers the 4th to 14th, the Council, Princes of Jerusalem confers the 15th and 16th, the Chapter of Rose Croix confers the 17th and 18th, and the Consistory confers the 19th to 32nd. Scottish rite Masons who have distinguished themselves in the cause of Masonry may receive the honorary 33rd degree; fewer than 8000 men hold this degree in the Northern and Southern jurisdictions together.

The Southern jurisdiction governs Valleys of this rite in thirty-five Southern and Western states, the District of Columbia, and United States territories and possessions; it claims more than 500,000 members. Slightly fewer belong to the Northern jurisdiction which operates in the fifteen other states.

One in ten Masons or about 400,000 belong to the York rite, sometimes known as the American rite. This rite culminates in the Knights Templar which is closed to Jews and other non-Christian Masons. The Mason who starts up the York ladder takes the degrees of Mark Master, Past Master, Most Excellent Master, and Royal Arch Mason. If he wishes he can take the Cryptic degrees of Royal Master, Select Master, and Super Excellent Master, or he can go directly on to the Order of the Red Cross, Order of the Knights of Malta, and Knights Templar.

Christian Masons who have been 32nd degree Masons or Knights Templar for five or more years may join the Royal Order of Scotland. Royal Arch Masons may become members of the degree of the Red Cross of Constantine. Knights Templar and 32nd degree Masons may join the "playground" of Freemasonry, the Ancient Arabic Order of Nobles of the Mystic Shrine.

Since each state grand lodge is independent it can determine the precise nature of its initiation ritual. Some grand lodges show traces of Antient or Modern influence going back to colonial times. The ritual and oaths of the lodges will vary somewhat from state to state but the essence of the Masonic ritual is the same.

The principal officers of a Masonic lodge are the Master, the Senior Warden, and the Junior Warden. Other officers include the secretary, treasurer, senior deacon, junior deacon, marshal, chaplain, stewards, and the tyler or doorkeeper.

Supposedly Masonry cannot recruit members; the initiative to join must come from the non-Mason. In the United States the applicant must be twenty-one or older, must declare his belief in a Supreme Being, must be of sound mind and body, and must be recommended by two Masons. Negroes or mulattoes are ineligible and in many states cripples may not be initiated. The initiation fee ranges from $50 to $75 for the three degrees of the Blue Lodge.

A committee investigates all candidates and makes a report at a regular meeting. Each applicant is voted upon by the brethren; if one blackball appears the vote is "cloudy" and a second vote is taken. If the candidate is again blackballed he is rejected, since the vote must be unanimous.

The lodge room should be located on the second or third floor of a building to discourage eavesdroppers. The interior of the Masonic lodge room features an altar in the center of the room on which rests a Bible and the square and compass. It is surrounded by three lighted tapers. A large letter "G" is suspended over the Master's chair; it stands for either Geometry or God, depending on the interpretation.

In the initiation to the first or Entered Apprentice degree the candidate is prepared by being divested of his coat, trousers, shoes, and socks. He must relinquish all metal objects such as coins and watches. The Junior Deacon gives him a pair of trousers and instructs him to put his left arm through the front of his shirt, exposing his left breast. The Deacon puts a slipper on his right foot, a blindfold over his eyes, and a blue silk rope called a cable tow around his neck.

The candidate is led to the door of the lodge room and the Junior Deacon gives three raps. Inside the Senior Deacon reports to the Master that there is an alarm at the inner door of the lodge. The Master tells him to find out the cause of the alarm and the Junior Deacon replies

"Mr. . . . . . ., a poor blind candidate, who has long been in darkness and now desires to be brought from darkness to light, by having and receiving a part of the light, rights, and benefits of this worshipful lodge, erected to God and dedicated to the Holy Saints John, as all brothers and fellows have done before."

After a series of questions whose answers are relayed to the Master, the Senior Deacon takes the compass from the altar. As the candidate enters the lodge room the Senior Deacon presses the point of the compass to the candidate's bare breast and declares:

> Mr. . . . . ., on entering this Lodge for the first time, I receive you on the point of a sharp instrument pressing your naked left breast, which is to teach you, as this is an instrument of torture to your flesh, so should the recollection of it ever be to your mind and conscience, should you attempt to reveal the secrets of Masonry unlawfully.

This ceremony is known as the "Shock of Entrance."

The candidate now kneels while the chaplain offers a prayer. He is asked in whom he puts his trust and he replies "In God." While he is led around the room and introduced to the lodge officers the Master reads Psalm 133. The Master offers some instruction:

> Freemasonry is a beautiful system of morals, veiled in allegory, and illustrated by symbols. Its tenets are brotherly love, relief and truth. Its cardinal virtues are temperance, fortitude, prudence, and justice. Its religion, if religion it may be called, is an unfeigned belief in the One Living and True God.

The nature of the solemn obligation is explained and the Master tells the candidate to kneel upon his left knee with the right hand resting on the Bible, square, and compass. He then repeats the oath of the first degree ending:

> To all of this and these I solemnly and sincerely promise and swear without equivocation, mental reservation, or

secret evasion in me whatever, binding myself under no less penalty than having my throat cut from end to end, my tongue torn out by its roots, and my body buried in the rough sands of the sea, a cabletow length from shore, where the tide ebbs and flows twice in 24 hours, should I knowingly or willingly violate this my solemn obligation as an apprentice. So help me God and enable me to keep steadfast in the due performance of the same.

The Master tells the candidate to kiss the Bible and tells the Senior Deacon to remove the cable tow. The Master asks what he most desires at this time and the candidate responds "Light!" At this the conductor jerks the blindfold off and the candidate sees the brothers of the lodge assembled for the first time.

The Master imparts the secret work of this first degree such as the symbolism of the Bible, square and compass, and the tapers. The name of the grip is given as Boaz. He presents the new Entered Apprentice with a white lambskin apron which is called "an emblem of innocence and the badge of a Mason."

He asks the new member for some metallic object which may be kept as a relic by the lodge. Of course, the candidate had to deposit all such items before he entered the lodge room. His inability to comply with the request is supposed to teach the lesson of charity. The candidate is now permitted to return to the preparation room and put on his street clothes. He returns and is told about the working tools of the first degree: a twenty-four-inch gauge and the common gavel. After the charge by the Master the first degree has been completed.

The candidate for the second or Fellow Craft degree is prepared much as he was for the first degree but this time he exposes his right arm and breast. The cable tow is wound twice around his arm and the slipper is worn on his left foot.

The routine at the lodge door is similar to that for the first degree but now the Senior Deacon places the square against the candidate's bare breast. The candidate repeats a second oath promising to observe secrecy, abide by the rules of the lodge, assist needy Fellow Crafts, and never cheat or defraud a Mason. This oath concludes with the penalty of "having my left breast torn open, my heart and vitals taken hence and given as a prey to the beasts of the field and the vultures of the air. . . ."

The new Fellow Craft tells the Master he seeks "Further light!" After instruction he receives the working tools of this degree: the plumb, square, and level. The pass grip of the Fellow Craft is "Shibboleth" and the name of the real grip is "Jachin."

Usually no more than three Fellow Crafts will be raised to the Master Mason degree in one evening. This degree is built around the legend of the assassination of Hiram Abiff.

This time the candidate rolls up his trousers on both legs and leaves his breast bare. He is blindfolded and the cable tow is wrapped around his waist three times. By giving the password "Tubal Cain" he is admitted to the lodge room. The Senior Deacon receives him with both points of the compass touching his breast. The Master Mason's oath follows:

I, ..., of my own free will and accord, in the presence of Almighty God, and this Worshipful Lodge, erected to Him and dedicated to the Holy Sts. John, do hereby and hereon most solemnly and sincerely promise and swear, that I will always hail, ever conceal, and never reveal any of the secrets, arts, parts, point or points, of the Master Masons' Degree, to any person or persons whomsoever, except that it be a true and lawful brother of this Degree, or in a regularly constituted Lodge of Master Masons, nor unto him, or them, until by strict trial, due examination, or lawful information, I shall have found him, or them, as lawfully entitled to the same as I am myself.

I furthermore promise and swear, that I will stand to and abide by all laws, rules, and regulations of the Master Masons' Degree, and of the Lodge of which I may hereafter become a member, as far as the same shall come to my knowledge; and that I will ever maintain and support the constitution, laws, and edicts of the Grand Lodge under which the same shall be holden.

Further, that I will acknowledge and obey all due signs and summonses sent to me from a Master Masons' Lodge, or given me by a brother of that Degree, if within the length of my cable tow.

Further, that I will always aid and assist all poor, distressed, worthy Master Masons, their widows and orphans, knowing them to be such, as far as their necessities may require, and my ability permit, without material injury to myself and family.

Further, that I will keep a worthy brother Master Mason's secrets inviolable, when communicated to and received by me as such, murder and treason excepted.

Further, that I will not aid, nor be present at, the initiation, passing, or raising of a woman, an old man in his dotage, a young man in his nonage, an atheist, a madman, or fool, knowing them to be such.

Further, that I will not sit in a Lodge of clandestine-made Masons, nor converse on the subject of Masonry with a clandestine-made Mason, nor one who has been expelled or suspended from a Lodge, while under that sentence, knowing him or them to be such.

Further, I will not cheat, wrong, nor defraud a Master Masons' Lodge, nor a brother of this Degree, knowingly, nor supplant him in any of his laudable undertakings, but will give him due and timely notice, that he may ward off all danger.

Further, that I will not knowingly strike a brother Master Mason, or otherwise do him personal violence in anger, except in the necessary defense of my family or property.

Further, that I will not have illegal carnal intercourse with a Master Mason's wife, his mother, sister, or daughter knowing them to be such, nor suffer the same to be done by others, if in my power to prevent.

Further, that I will not give the Grand Masonic word, in any other manner or form than that in which I shall receive it, and then in a low breath.

Further, that I will not give the Grand Hailing Sign of

Distress except in case of the most imminent danger, in a just and lawful Lodge, or for the benefit of instruction; and if ever I should see it given, or hear the words accompanying it, by a worthy brother in distress, I will fly to his relief, if there is a greater probability of saving his life than losing my own.

All this I most solemnly, sincerely promise and swear, with a firm and steady resolution to perform the same, without any hesitation, myself, under no less penalty than that of having my body severed in two, my bowels taken from thence and burned to ashes, the ashes scattered before the four winds of heaven, that no more remembrance might be had of so vile and wicked a wretch as I would be, should I ever, knowingly, violate this my Master Mason's obligation. So help me God, and keep me steadfast in the due performance of the same.

After repeating the oath he kisses the Bible. The cable tow is removed and he answers "More light!" when asked what he desires most. The working tools are explained, especially the trowel, and the candidate is allowed to get dressed in his usual clothes as the lodge takes an intermission.

Welcomed back to the lodge room by his brothers he is told that he is not yet through with this degree. The Senior Deacon will guide him through the rest of the ordeal. The lodge sings a stanza of *Nearer, My God, to Thee* and the candidate is ordered to pray. He will become Hiram Abiff in the playlet to follow although the Senior Deacon will speak his lines.

According to the legend, which does not appear in the Bible, only three people knew the secret Masonic word: Hiram Abiff, King Solomon, and Hiram, the King of Tyre. Three ruffians want to obtain the word from Hiram Abiff. They corner him in the temple and when he refuses to disclose the word they kill and bury him. The other Masons discover the body as well as the three murderers who are executed.

Attempts are made to raise Hiram Abiff from the dead. One tries to raise him with the grip of the Entered Apprentice and another with the Fellow Craft grip. They fail because "the skin slips from the flesh" and "the flesh cleaves not to the bone." Finally an attempt is made to raise him on the five points of fellowship: foot to foot, knee to knee, breast to breast, hand to back, and mouth to ear. The Master whispers the grand Masonic word — "Ma-hah-bone" — and the candidate is "resurrected."

The symbolism in the degree is explained and the action is recapitulated. This concludes the third degree. The candidate is now a full-fledged Mason.

Two major reasons account for the opposition to Freemasonry of various Christian denominations. The first objection has been that Masonry presents itself as a religion of naturalism.

In his *Morals and Dogma* Albert Pike declared, "Every Masonic lodge is a temple of religion; and its teachings are instruction in religion" (p. 213). The Masonic encyclopedist Albert Mackey stated:

> Look at its ancient landmarks, its sublime ceremonies, its profound symbols and allegories — all inculcating religious observance, and teaching religious truth, and who can deny that it is eminently a religious institution. . . ? Masonry, then, is indeed a religious institution; and on this ground mainly, if not alone, should the religious Mason defend it (*Encyclopedia of Freemasonry,* p. 619).

The "light" which the Mason receives in his lodge is not the light of the revealed truths of the Gospel. Masonry ignores the central doctrines of the Christian Church: the Trinity, the fall and redemption of man, the necessity of baptism, the role of the sacraments, the Church. It refers to itself as a religious institution but the religion it offers its adherents is not Christianity but a basic deism with a few Christian overtones. But for many men the lodge offers practically everything they would find in a church: temples and altars, a moral code, feast days, vestments, prayers, initiation and burial rites, worship, the promise of an afterlife, and the like.

The second major religious objection to Masonry is that the lodge has no right to administer solemn oaths as part of its initiation ceremonies. The Church or State may require swearing such oaths for a serious reason but the preservation of Masonic secrets hardly qualifies as a serious reason. Any scholar can soon discover all he wants to know about the secret passwords, rituals, grips, etc., of the lodge. No one should agree to self-destruction to keep secrets which are not secrets at all and call upon God as a witness.

Christian objections also include the possible subversion of the State, which some Masonic bodies have attempted, the fostering of religious indifference, the long history of anti-Catholicism of the Grand Orients, and the racism of American Masonry. Lutherans and some other Protestants find that the lodge offers "salvation by character" instead of the justification by faith alone which they see as the central Christian proclamation.

Pope Clement XII issued the first bull against Freemasonry on April 28, 1738, only twenty-one years after the founding of the Grand Lodge of England. Benedict XIV confirmed this prohibition in 1751 and since then six other popes have spelled out the Catholic position regarding the Masonic lodge. The most famous encyclical on the subject was *Humanum genus* issued by Leo XIII in 1894. The prohibition is now part of the canon law of the Church (Canon 2335).

In brief the Church declares that no Catholic may join the Masonic lodge or any affiliated Masonic organization (such as the Eastern Star or DeMolay) without incurring excommunication reserved in a simple manner to the Holy

See. Such an excommunicated person may not receive the sacraments, share in the spiritual treasures of the Church, receive a Christian burial or be buried in consecrated ground, or act as a godfather in baptism. A Freemason who wishes to enter the Catholic Church must first sever all connections with the lodge.

A partial listing of the Eastern Orthodox and Protestant churches which also forbid or discourage lodge membership is given in Part I, "The World of Secret Organizations." The National Christian Association of Chicago coordinates Protestant opposition to the lodges and publishes the *Christian Cynosure.* All told the majority of the world's Christians belong to denominations which forbid dual membership in the Church and the lodge.

Although the Second Vatican Council established new bench marks in the ecumenical movement which looks forward to the reunion of Christians, it made no moves to soften the Church's stand against Masonry. The subject came up only once in Council discussions; a Mexican bishop suggested that friendlier relations be promoted between Catholics and Masons.

At the close of the Council Pope Paul VI declared a jubilee year to begin on January 1, 1966. During these months the Pope granted the power to confessors to absolve from censures and ecclesiastical penalties those who have joined a Masonic lodge provided that the penitent withdraws completely from the lodge and promises to repair and prevent, insofar as he can, any scandal or harm. The confessor was asked to impose a "grave and salutary" penance commensurate with the gravity of the offense. After the jubilee the lifting of the penalty of excommunication would again be reserved to the Holy See.

Here and there in the United States some efforts have been made to breach the wall of prejudice between Catholics and Masons. Bishops and priests have been invited to address Masonic gatherings; joint social affairs have been sponsored by Knights of Columbus councils and Masonic lodges.

Not many Catholics foresee any change in the bar against Catholic membership in Masonic lodges. One of the few Catholic scholars to propose a change in the present prohibition has been Father John A. O'Brien of the University of Notre Dame. Writing in the December, 1965 edition of the *Indiana Freemason* Father O'Brien declared: "I earnestly hope that conferences will be held between the representatives of Freemasonry and the Catholic Church which will lead to the removal of the Church's ban. . . . The circumstances which prompted the prohibition in the Old World seem to have little, if any, relevance to the American scene. I can not but regard it as unfortunate, unnatural and pathological that the members of the largest religious body in the United States may not be active members of the nation's largest fraternal organization."

Supreme Knight John W. McDevitt of the Knights of Columbus asserted in February, 1966 that "it is high time for the dissipation of any recriminations, disaffections or petty jealousies that may have formed a barrier to cooperation and friendship between the K of C and Masons." He spoke at a breakfast meeting jointly sponsored by the K of C and Freemasons. He declared that the Knights "are eager to extend to brothers of the Masonic order an embrace of friendship, understanding, trust and charity that will bring us to new heights of ecumenism in fraternalism."

Since the basic objection of the Church to Freemasonry is not that the lodge is anticlerical but that it proposes a religion of naturalism and imposes an unlawful solemn oath, few Roman Catholics see any likelihood that either Masonry or the Church will change its stand. This does not mean that the two institutions must foster a mutual hostility or tolerate vilification of each other.

Freemasonry faces serious problems in the years ahead. The lodges are not recruiting the young college graduates, most of whom see little value in such membership. Too many Blue Lodges serve merely as stepping-stones to the Scottish rite and the Shrine. Attendance in the larger lodges sometimes falls below even ten percent of the membership. American Masonry has not been able to modify its increasingly anachronistic racial bias. World Masonry, like Christianity, is fragmented and unity seems to be as elusive as ever; the United Grand Lodge of England and the Anglo-Saxon lodges form the largest group of Masons but there are also the Masons of the various Grand Orients, the Prince Hall Masons, and the independent Masonic jurisdictions.

(See **Acacia, Order of Amaranth, DeMolay, Order of the Eastern Star, Grotto, Job's Daughters, Negro lodges, Rainbow Girls, Sciots, Shrine, Tall Cedars of Lebanon,** and **White Shrine**)

Good Templars
(International Order of Good Templars)

At one time hundreds of thousands of Americans, usually fired by religious zeal, gave their allegiance to a variety of temperance lodges. One of the few surviving temperance lodges is the International Order of Good Templars and its membership has declined drastically in recent decades. Stevens estimated the number of Good Templars in the United States in 1907 at 350,000; the total membership in this country had fallen to 3000 in 1965.

The Order was founded in Utica, New York, in 1851 as a revised version of the men-only Knights of Jericho. It expanded rapidly after the Civil War but the defeat of prohibition doomed the temperance lodge as a force in American life.

G

The Good Templars lodge was introduced into England in 1868 and into Sweden shortly thereafter. Today the Swedish Grand Lodge enrolls more members than any other nation. Lodges can also be found in Canada, Austria, Denmark, Finland, France, Germany, Greece, Iceland, Ireland, the Netherlands, Norway, Scotland, Switzerland, Turkey, Wales, Nigeria, Liberia, India, Japan, Australia, and several other nations. The United States lodges show a distinctly Scandinavian flavor; the lodges in several states use the Swedish language in conducting meetings.

Membership is open to both men and women; the Order also sponsors the International Good Templar Youth Federation. There are no racial or religious restrictions but all members must pledge total abstinence from intoxicating liquor. The Good Templars also promote world peace, racial equality, and the United Nations. It declares: "We believe in a sober warless world and dedicate ourselves to its achievement" and "We believe in total abstinence as the best means toward social and cultural progress." The lodge urges national prohibition, encourages men and women to take the pledge, and engages in temperance education.

A 1965 statement of the International Grand Lodge states: "The International Order of Good Templars, being the first international movement, apart from the Churches, organized on a basis of equal rights for all races, still vigorously upholds its tradition of opposition to racial prejudice and discrimination." It condemns the apartheid policies of South Africa and applauds the civil rights movement in the United States.

The Holy Office condemned the Order of Good Templars on August 9, 1893, but gave no specific reason for its stand. It attached no canonical penalties for joining but sought to discourage Roman Catholics from affiliating with this lodge.

Other temperance lodges which once exerted a strong

influence in American communities and which are now dead or moribund are the Sons of Temperance, the Independent Order of Good Samaritans and Daughters of Samaria, and the Rechabites.

Grotto
(Mystic Order of Veiled Prophets of the Enchanted Realm)

Master Masons may join one of two fun organizations open to Masons of their rank: the Mystic Order of Veiled Prophets of the Enchanted Realm or the Tall Cedars of Lebanon. Both orders imitate the Shrine but offer the chance to relax and cut up at far less cost than the Shrine initiation and dues.

The Grotto is the most common name for the M.O.V.P.E.R. The Order was founded in 1889 in Hamilton, New York as the Fairchild Deviltry Committee. Until 1904 Grottos were chartered only in the state of New York but since then the Grotto has spread to most of the states of the union and to some Canadian provinces. Each city can have no more than one Grotto. Total membership exceeds 100,000.

The ritual is supposedly "founded on a very ancient Persian manuscript, discovered in a secret vault in one of the sacred temples of Teheran, the City of Mystery." It was revised in 1940 by Americans rather than Persians.

Ferguson remarks: "The Grotto attempts to rival the inspired absurdities of the Shrine, but its costumes and lingo have a more fabricated and stilted quality, not unlike the top-lofty whimsies of a high school fraternity" (*Fifty Million Brothers*, p. 318).

The ladies who comprise the Daughters of Mokanna

auxiliary have been assisting the men of the Grotto since 1919. An elected Mighty Chosen One heads the local Caldrons of this Order.

Hibernians
(Ancient Order of Hibernians)

Calling itself the oldest Catholic lay organization in America, the Ancient Order of Hibernians limits its membership to men of Irish birth or descent, through either parent. In addition the applicants must be practicing Roman Catholics, over sixteen and under forty-five years of age, and in good health.

Although the AOH was organized in the United States on May 4, 1836, in New York City, the founding of the Order has been placed as early as 1565 in Ireland. In those days the Catholic priest was a hunted man. The English rulers forbade the celebration of Mass and the education of Irish children in the tenets of the Catholic faith. To protect the priesthood and preserve the practice of their religion certain Irishmen formed themselves into groups of Ribbonmen, the forerunners of the Hibernians.

Besides trying to maintain the ancient religion the Hibernians sought to remedy the injustices perpetrated by the English landlords. In a sense they were Irish vigilantes. In the nineteenth century the Ribbonmen sent warning letters to offending landlords; these letters were often signed with the name of the widow Molly Maguire who had been evicted from her cottage by a heartless landlord.

When Wolf Tone proclaimed a free and independent Ireland in 1798 the Ancient Order of Hibernians rallied to the cause. Through the years they continued to support a free Ireland and still urge the incorporation of the six northeastern counties into the Republic of Ireland.

At the time the AOH was introduced in this country the Catholic Church had become the object of persecution and even physical attack by certain nativist organizations. In New York City the Hibernians defended the churches from the attempted arson of Know-Nothing bands. While they were guarding church buildings from marauding Know-Nothings, Archbishop Hughes was warning: "If a single Catholic church is burned in New York City, the city will become a second Moscow."

By 1853 the Ancient Order of Hibernians was strong enough to mass 12,000 members in the annual St. Patrick's Day parade, and by 1868 the number of paraders exceeded 40,000.

Between 1862 and 1876 the secret apparatus of the AOH was employed by disgruntled miners in the Pennsylvania coal fields in an effort to better oppressive working conditions. The coal barons hired thousands of Irish immigrants to work in the mines, paying low wages for hard and hazardous work. They gave little thought to safety; in 1869 at the Avondale mine 179 miners were burned alive in a mine fire; the pit had only one airway and one entrance. The owners battled all attempts to organize the miners into labor unions and blacklisted anyone thought engaged in labor agitation.

The AOH provided the secrecy, passwords, meeting places for the men seeking better conditions in the mines. Those Hibernians actively engaged in these labor battles were known as the Molly Maguires. All the Mollies were Hibernians but not all the Hibernians were Mollies; no formal connection existed between the two. Nevertheless the AOH was eventually blamed for the arson, sabotage, murders, and whippings engineered by the Molly Maguires in this part of the country.

To destroy the Mollies the owners hired the Pinkerton

detective agency and put up a reward of $100,000 to any-
one who could furnish inside information on the terrorists.
Their most successful spy was James McParlan who claimed
he had been a member of the AOH in Buffalo and gained
acceptance among the Molly Maguires in 1873. His testi-
mony in 1876–1877 helped convict eleven Mollies of murder. Those hanged wore roses to the scaffold. All in all
nineteen Mollies were hanged, many others were sent to
prison, and the Molly Maguires were broken.

At its 1876 national convention the Ancient Order of
Hibernians repudiated the activities of the Molly Maguires
but the reputation of the Order was tarnished. A later
reform minimized the possibility that the AOH could ever
again be used as a cover for terrorist plots. Dissatisfied
members formed a schismatic Ancient Order of Hibernians
Board of Erin in 1884 but the schism was healed in 1898.

Today the AOH is organized along the same lines as
most other American fraternal societies. It seeks to promote "friendship, unity, and Christian charity among its
members." Its lodge emblems include the harp, shamrock,
clasped hands, and three links. The AOH not only promotes social activities but fosters patriotism, the cause of
Irish independence, and an understanding of the ideals, history, and traditions of the Irish people.

Local units are known as Divisions. They have authority
to fix initiation fees, monthly dues, sick and death benefits.
County, state, district, provincial, and national officers complete the organization. In 1965 membership of the Ancient
Order of Hibernians was given as 181,000. An auxiliary,
the Daughters of Erin, was organized in 1894. The AOH
publishes the bimonthly *National Hibernian Digest*.

Since its founding the Order has distributed about $27,-
000,000 in sick benefits, $13,000,000 in death benefits,
and $10,000,000 for various charitable purposes. It has
donated $50,000 for a chair of Celtic languages at the

Catholic University of America and has made other contributions to victims of earthquakes and floods, the Irish College in Rome, and the Catholic Church Extension Society. The Hibernians have made substantial gifts to the missions in China, India, and Burma staffed by the Columban Fathers. In 1960 the AOH broadened its mission fund to include the Irish Carmelite missions and Catholic missions in Africa.

Cardinal Spellman serves as national chaplain; Cardinals Cushing and McIntyre also hold membership in the Order.

President John F. Kennedy joined the Ancient Order of Hibernians in 1947.

Job's Daughters

Teen-age girls who are related to Master Masons may apply for membership in Job's Daughters. They must be between thirteen and twenty years of age, possess a good moral character, believe in God, in the Ten Commandments, and in the Lord's Prayer.

The founder chose the name of the organization from a passage in the Bible: "And in all the land there were no women so fair as the daughters of Job" (Job 42:15). Mrs. Ethel T. W. Mick, a member of the Eastern Star and wife of a prominent Omaha physician, founded Job's Daughters in 1921. LeRoy T. Wilcox, active in Masonic circles in Chicago, wrote the ritual, constitution, and bylaws of the organization.

National headquarters remains in Omaha. The Order is composed of the national supreme guardian council and local Bethels. At present there are about 1600 Bethels in the United States, Canada, Australia, and the Philippines, with 150,000 members.

It takes twenty girls to form a Bethel and nineteen serve as elected or appointed officers. The chief officers are the honored queen, senior princess, junior princess, guide, marshal, and chaplain. According to the ritual the duty of the chaplain is to "preside at the Altar during the devotions of the Bethel and to communicate the pledge to Pilgrims. The significance of her duty is that piety, religion, and reverence for sacred things are the beacon lights of life."

During initiations and meetings the officers are clothed in white Grecian robes with white or purple cinctures. The emblems of the Order are the white dove, urn of incense, lilies of the valley, and horn of plenty.

Only members of Job's Daughters, parents or guardians of members, and properly qualified Masons or members of the Eastern Star may witness a meeting or initiation ritual. Early in the ceremony the guide and the marshal escort any new guests to the altar. There the chaplain administers the following pledge:

> In the presence of these witnesses I solemnly affirm on my honor that I will never divulge the transactions of any Bethel of Job's Daughters or the ritualistic ceremony of the Order or any part of either to anyone who is not lawfully entitled thereto, that I will encourage the fidelity of all members of Job's Daughters by a faithful observance of this pledge.

In the initiation itself the honored queen asks the inner guard if there are any pilgrims waiting for entrance. The marshal and guide conduct the pilgrims into the Bethel. The honored queen later in the ritual reminds the pilgrims: "We are all daughters of one God, and by the most intimate ties we are related to the Masonic fraternity, that organization which stands for brotherhood of humanity." The initiation includes a typical oath or obligation.

Like the parallel Rainbow Girls the Job's Daughters Order was organized by Masons or wives of Masons. It seeks to cement ties between the girls who join and the Masonic fraternity so that eventually the girls will want to join the Order of the Eastern Star.

Occasionally Catholic young ladies seek to join the Job's Daughters since their fathers or other relatives are Master Masons. As a part of the Masonic system Job's Daughters falls under the same condemnation as the Masonic lodge itself. Girls cannot belong to Job's Daughters and the Catholic Church at the same time.

Junior Order United American Mechanics

A relic of the nativist movement of the 1840's and 1850's, the Junior Order United American Mechanics is an offshoot of an earlier organization of white Protestant workingmen who opposed the further immigration of Irish and Germans and the spread of Roman Catholicism. A small band of such workingmen met in a grocery store in Philadelphia in 1845 and formed a society they called the Union of Workers.

This name was later changed to the Order of United American Mechanics. Only native white Americans could join the Order and they also had to profess belief in a Supreme Being and in the separation of Church and State; men engaged in the liquor business were ruled out.

In 1853 the lodge authorized establishment of a branch for younger men which came to be known as the Junior Order United American Mechanics. The junior branch soon outstripped the parent body and declared its independence in 1885. Today only the Junior Order survives; it enrolls men and women of all ages and has no particular appeal to mechanics as such.

The JOUAM frankly espoused the cause of the Protestant workingman against the supposed threat of immigrants, especially Roman Catholics, who might compete for their jobs. An early statement of purposes of the lodge read:

> To maintain and promote the interest of Americans, and shield them from the depressing effects of foreign competition; to assist Americans in obtaining employment; to encourage Americans in business; to establish a sick and funeral fund; to maintain the public school system of the United States of America, to prevent sectarian interference therewith, and uphold the reading of the Holy Bible therein.

The JOUAM urged an end to immigration and declared that it stood "for the public school with the American flag over it, and against the union of church and state." Its enthusiasm for Bible reading in the public schools may have been motivated by Catholic objections to the prevalent use of the King James version. Members of the lodge were usually active in the Know-Nothing movement and were instrumental in organizing the anti-Catholic American Protective Association.

Today the national secretary of the Junior Order United American Mechanics reports that the organization has no restrictions against membership by Roman Catholics, Jews, or Negroes. Although it has traditionally defended the Protestant faith, its rituals include no prayers in the name of Jesus Christ. A chaplain opens each meeting with Scripture reading and closes with prayer. Initiates swear an oath in the secret initiation; the lodge provides a burial service for those who request it.

A ladies auxiliary was formed in 1875 but abandoned. Now the Junior Order declares itself "open to American citizens of both sexes and to all ages from the cradle onward." Although it claimed more than 160,000 members at the turn of the century, the Junior Order reported 40,000 members in 1965. There are 1000 councils or lodges in twenty-seven states.

Members pay for a small life insurance policy as part of their dues. For example, an applicant between thirty-one and forty receives a $400 policy. The lodge sponsors a legal reserve insurance department with over $25,000,-000 in force. It has paid more than $61,000,000 in benefits since its founding in 1899.

Knights of Columbus

During the heyday of secret societies in the latter part of the nineteenth century many Roman Catholic men began to long for a fraternity which would receive the approval of the Church. The Ancient Order of Hibernians limited membership to Irishmen and other fraternal societies enrolled Catholics of a particular nationality. A few Catholics defied the Church by joining the condemned Masonic lodge.

The need for a secret society open to all Catholic men was seen by the Reverend Michael J. McGivney, the twenty-nine-year-old curate at St. Mary's parish in New Haven, Connecticut. He began to meet in the rectory with a handful of men of the parish to devise such a society which would combine the social benefits of Freemasonry with the protection of insurance. At first they suggested that their new society be called the "Sons of Columbus" but later settled upon "Knights of Columbus." They received a charter from the state on March 29, 1882.

Today the Knights of Columbus enrolls 1,177,154 members in 5225 councils. With assets in excess of $260,000,-000 it has written insurance in the amount of $1,500,-000,000 on its members. The Order paid $892 to the beneficiary of its first deceased member in 1884; total benefits paid since then have been more than $177,-

000,000. The K of C has become the largest fraternal benefit society of Roman Catholic men in the world.

The charter set forth the aims of the new society which were: (a) rendering pecuniary aid to its members and beneficiaries of members; (b) rendering mutual aid and assistance to its sick and disabled members; (c) promoting such social and cultural intercourse as shall be desirable and proper; and (d) promoting and conducting educational, charitable, religious, social welfare, war relief, and welfare and public relief work.

Like almost all secret societies the Knights of Columbus looked to the Masonic lodge for its model. It constructed a three-degree system with the usual passwords, signs, and grips. It did not extract a solemn oath or obligation but asked its initiates to keep the secrets of the ceremonies under a gentlemen's agreement. Unlike Freemasonry and Odd Fellowship, it provided a full line of insurance policies.

The English Masonic author of *Light Invisible* labels the Knights of Columbus as Catholic Freemasonry and comments: "At best this organization can only be described as a consolation prize for the good boys who might otherwise be tempted into Freemasonry" (p. 110, London, Regency Press, 1952).

An additional fourth degree was introduced in 1900. Since the Catholic Church was often viewed with suspicion as a foreign institution and possibly a subversive one, the motif chosen for this degree was patriotism. Members of fourth-degree assemblies wear uniforms similar to those of an admiral with plumed hat, sword, cape, and baldric. They sometimes form an escort for religious processions.

The only auxiliary sponsored by the Knights of Columbus is the Columbian Squires for young men. The first circle was established in Duluth, Minnesota, in 1925; today there are about 700 Columbian Squires circles. A number of independent women's organizations work with local K of C councils such as the Daughters of Isabella (120,000 members) but they enjoy no official recognition.

During World War I the Knights of Columbus engaged in extensive morale building work among American troops. They operated five K of C huts in London and forty-five in France. After the war many ex-servicemen joined the Order and helped swell its membership.

At the start of World War II the K of C's again expressed an interest in carrying on these overseas activities but the hierarchy decided otherwise. The American bishops set up the National Catholic Community Service to coordinate services for the members of the armed forces. The Knights reluctantly accepted this decision but a statement in a K of C booklet reveals their disappointment:

> The effect of this decision was to exclude the Knights of Columbus as an organization from performing a service for the armed forces of the United States in the second World War such as had brought it world-wide fame in connection with the first World War (*These Men They Call Knights,* p. 15).

Although the primary purpose of the Knights of Columbus has always been to provide insurance protection for Catholic men, the Order has also engaged in many charitable and religious activities. Not long after its founding it contributed $50,000 for a chair in American history at the Catholic University of America and in 1907 it raised $500,000 to provide scholarships at the University. These grants have helped 450 men obtain an education.

Local K of C councils contribute to boys' homes, Newman centers, hospitals, Catholic colleges and universities. Among the larger K of C projects have been the $1,000,000 campanile at the National Shrine in Washington, D. C., and the Vatican Microfilm Library at St. Louis University.

A large-scale effort to interest non-Catholics in the

Catholic religion was launched in 1948. The K of C began to insert paid advertisements in secular newspapers and magazines. The ads invited readers to send for free religious pamphlets and to enroll in a correspondence course in Catholicism. Since the start of this ad program more than 5,200,000 people have requested pamphlets and 565,000 have enrolled in the courses. Four priests and thirty-five lay people handle the daily mail which averages 1200 letters and postcards. This program costs each Knight about eighty cents a year.

The Knights of Columbus have been the victims of one of the most widespread libels in modern times, almost rivaling the anti-Semitic Protocols of the Elders of Zion. This is the bogus oath supposedly taken by initiates of the fourth degree. It started circulation in 1912.

In its classic form the spurious oath begins:

> I . . . now in the presence of Almighty God, the Blessed Virgin Mary, the Blessed St. John the Baptist, the Holy Apostles, St. Peter and St. Paul, and all the Saints, sacred host of Heaven, and to you, my ghostly father, the Society of of Jesus, founded by Ignatius Loyola, in the pontification of Paul III, and continued to the present, do by the womb of the Virgin, the matrix of God, and the rod of Jesus Christ, declare and swear that His Holiness, the Pope, is Christ's vice-regent, and is the true and only head of the Catholic Church throughout the earth. . . .

The oath continues:

> I do further promise and declare that I will, when opportunity presents, make and wage relentless war, secretly and openly against all heretics, Protestants and Masons, as I am directed to do to extirpate them from the face of the whole earth; that I will spare neither age, sex, nor condition; that I will hang, burn, waste, boil, flay, strangle and bury alive those infamous heretics; rip up the stomachs, and wombs of their women, and crush their infants' heads against the walls, in order to annihilate their execrable race. That when the

same cannot be done openly I will secretly use the poison cup, the strangulation cord, the steel of the poniard, or the leaden bullet.

That anyone could accept this as genuine demonstrates the depth of anti-Catholicism in certain circles in the United States. A member of the Knights of Columbus who was defeated for public office claimed that the bogus oath had been a factor in his defeat. When a committee on elections reprinted the oath in the Congressional Record to show its falsity, the perpetrators of the libel added to the printing of the oath "Copied from the Congressional Record, Feb. 15, 1913" and led naïve readers to suppose that this gave it official standing.

The K of C turned over a complete set of their ritual work and pledges to a committee of prominent Freemasons. This Masonic committee investigated the bogus oath and declared:

> Neither the alleged oath nor any oath or pledge bearing the remotest resemblance thereto in matter, manner, spirit or purpose is used or forms a part of the ceremonies of any degree of the Knights of Columbus. The alleged oath is scurrilous, wicked and libelous and must be the invention of an impious and venomous mind . . . There is no propaganda proposed or taught against Protestants or Masons or persons not of the Catholic faith. Indeed, Protestants and Masons are not referred to directly or indirectly in the ceremonials or pledges . . . We can find nothing in the entire ceremonials of the Order that to our minds could be objected to by any person.

For twenty-five years the Knights of Columbus have offered $25,000 to anyone who will prove that the oath is now or ever was taken by a Knight of Columbus, that Protestants or Masons are even mentioned in any K of C ceremonial. No one has collected the reward. In a series of lawsuits the Knights have obtained injunctions against the circulation of the oath and judgments of criminal libel. The most recent was an injunction against a woman and a Baptist minister in district court in Wilson, North Carolina, in 1963.

The Knights of Columbus publish *Columbia* magazine which goes each month to members of the Order. This gives it the largest circulation of any Catholic periodical in the United States.

In the field of political and social action the Knights have engaged in campaigns to prevent Marshall Tito from visiting this country, to enforce sanctions against the anticlerical governments of Mexico in the 1930's, and to insert the phrase "under God" in the pledge of allegiance. Various councils have sponsored anti-Communist forums and the current national K of C effort is directed against pornography.

Unlike Freemasonry and most of the lodges the Knights of Columbus admit men regardless of race. Until 1964, however, as few as five bigoted members of a council could blackball a Negro applicant. Now an applicant may be turned down only if one third of the members present at the meeting reject him. Thousands of Catholic Negroes belong to the Knights of Columbus and a few have served as Grand Knights of their councils.

Membership is open to Catholic men over the age of eighteen. Those who cannot pass the physical examination or who do not wish to buy insurance may join as associate members to enjoy the social privileges of the Order. Councils have been chartered in every state of the union and in Canada, Puerto Rico, Mexico, and the Philippines.

Councils enforce no attendance requirements so that it is possible for a man to receive the initiation degrees and remain a member in good standing for the rest of his life by simply mailing in his dues. In many councils only ten to 15 percent of the membership shows up for a regular meeting although larger turnouts can be expected for banquets, dances, and other social affairs. This relatively low participation in the everyday work of the council is the pattern of most Masonic and other lodges as well.

Supreme Knight John W. McDevitt declared in 1965 that the K of C's welcome "honest criticism from inside and outside the order." He said that in seeking renewal of the organization the Knights did not intend to "abandon wisdom and prudence to the fever of enthusiasm for change."

Other fraternal benefit societies for Catholics include the Catholic Daughters of America (215,000 members), Catholic Knights of America (15,889), Catholic Knights of St. George (17,773), Catholic Women's Benevolent Legion (4000), Czech Catholic Union of Texas (12,875), First Catholic Slovak Ladies' Union (91,063), Knights of St. John, Ladies Catholic Benevolent Association (76,009), Lithuanian Roman Catholic Alliance of America, and Women's Catholic Order of Foresters (91,495).

Knights of the Golden Eagle

The pageantry of the Crusades provided the inspiration for the Knights of the Golden Eagle which was founded by John E. Burbage of Baltimore in 1873. He wanted to form a secret fraternity which would "go hand in hand with religion" and this society retains a strong evangelical Protestant flavor. One of its recruiting pamphlets states that it "demands unswerving belief in the work, the teachings and the mission of Christ." Oaths are sworn on an open Bible.

The stated object of the Knights of the Golden Eagle is "to unite white male persons of good moral character." It offers sick and funeral benefits. Members take the three degrees of Pilgrim, Knight, and Crusader.

Knights meet in local Castles governed by state Grand

Castles. The Order once counted 60,000 Knights but now reports a membership of only 15,000, mostly in Pennsylvania. An official pamphlet explains: "The growth has been gradual and natural. No strenuous effort has ever been made to expand it." Women may join the auxiliary organization, the Ladies of the Golden Eagle. National headquarters is in North Wales, Pennsylvania.

Knights of Malta

Taking its inspiration from the Loyal Orange Institution the Ancient and Illustrious Order Knights of Malta "welcomes all Protestants, by whatever name known, who love our Lord Jesus Christ, to enlist under its banner." Like the Orangemen the Knights of Malta express their Protestantism by an aggressive anti-Catholicism. They exclude from membership any Protestant who is married to a Roman Catholic.

The Knights of Malta defines itself as

a body of men, banded together, under most binding forms, to comfort one another in the practice of the Christian religion; to offer mutual assistance in time of need; to promote Protestant unity; to defend the Protestant faith against all foes whatsoever; to ever defend civil and religious liberty; to exercise the fullest toleration and charity toward all men; to practice benevolence; and to maintain a universal Protestant fraternity.

This Order was introduced into the United States in 1870 and underwent a reorganization in 1889. It worked twelve degrees. During the 1920's the Knights of Malta claimed 75,000 members but this number has dropped to a fraction of that figure. (This lodge should not be confused with the Order of Knights of Malta which forms one of the degrees of the York rite of Freemasonry.)

Knights of Peter Claver

Most of the members of the Knights of Peter Claver are Roman Catholics of the Negro race. This Order was founded in 1909 by four Josephite priests (Fathers Conrad Rebeshler, John Dorsey, Samuel Kelly, and Joseph Van Baast) and three Catholic laymen (Gilbert Faustina, Frank Collins, and Frank Trenier). It was incorporated in Mobile, Alabama, in 1911. At that time the major Catholic fraternal societies would not accept Negro members.

In 1917 the Knights established a Junior Knights order for boys under eighteen as well as a fourth-degree division. The Ladies Auxiliary was organized in 1922 and the Junior Daughters for girls under eighteen was begun in 1930. Since 1964 men over fifty-five have been allowed to join the Knights of Peter Claver as associate members.

The Order encourages Catholic Action and parish activities, provides financial assistance to sick members and to beneficiaries, awards scholarships, fosters recreation and fellowship. The designated beneficiary receives up to $1,000 on the death of a member. The councils themselves pay a small sick benefit each week.

The Knights of Peter Claver occupies the Claver Building in New Orleans and reports assets of over $1,000,000. The membership was more than 17,000 in 1965. Each member receives the bimonthly *Claverite*.

Knights of Pythias

In many respects the Knights of Pythias can serve as a textbook example of the decline of fraternalism in American life. The once mighty K of P lodge reported 908,000 members in 1923 but today it would be hard pressed to muster 200,000 Knights in the Castles of the Order.

Justus H. Rathbone and six other government clerks founded the Knights of Pythias in Washington, D. C., on February 15, 1864. Rathbone had once directed a school play by the Irish poet and dramatist John Banim which told the story of Damon and Pythias. These two natives of Syracuse who lived some 400 years before Christ exemplified the highest ideals of human friendship.

The founder of the new lodge drew on this story for his ritual and borrowed elements also from some of the other lodges to which he belonged including the Masons and Red Men. The Knights of Pythias sputtered and died within six months of its founding and Rathbone resigned as Venerable Patriarch. He reconsidered his action, however, and rejoined the remnants of the lodge. The founder revised his ritual and by 1868 there were about 3000 Knights in several states.

Things would not run smoothly for the fledgling society. The District of Columbia lodge authorized Rathbone to compose a new and higher degree. Only those who had completed the degrees of Page, Esquire, and Knight would be eligible to take the degree admitting them to the Supreme Order of Pythian Knighthood. Instead of welcoming this new degree the Supreme Lodge met in 1869 and strictly forbade any Knight of Pythias to take the degree under threat of explusion.

For the second time Rathbone quit the lodge. He tried to nurse his Supreme Order of Pythian Knighthood along but it did not prosper. Finally in 1874 the founder of the K of P asked to return to membership and was readmitted after some debate. The Knights recognized him as founder of the Order and gave him the job of lecturer. After ten years in the role he was again in severe financial trouble; the Knights passed the hat and raised $5,085 for Rathbone.

By the end of the nineteenth century the Knights of Pythias lodge was booming. More than half a million American men had joined the Order. Hundreds and even thousands marched down the main streets of American cities wearing the military costume of the Uniform Rank. An Endowment Rank which provided insurance benefits was established in 1877. (The insurance department was separated from the lodge in 1931; insurance for members is now provided by the United Mutual Life Insurance Company.)

Any white man who believed in a Supreme Being and was in good health could apply for membership. Negroes applied for and were refused membership in the lodge in 1869. Using a pirated ritual they formed their own "Knights of Pythias of North and South America, Europe, Asia and Africa."

Most of the top Pythians were also Freemasons and often held membership in additional lodges such as the Odd Fellows and Red Men. President Franklin D. Roosevelt was initiated into the Knights of Pythias in 1936 in a special ceremony in the diplomatic reception room of the White House. His enrollment hardly compensated for the loss of members during the Depression years; in one two-year period more than 125,000 Knights abandoned their Castles.

A cluster of affiliated organizations grew up around the main Order. Serving the same fun purpose as the Grotto, Tall Cedars of Lebanon, and the Shrine, the Dramatic Order Knights of Khorassan was organized in 1894, presided over by a "Most Worthy and Illustrious Imperial Prince." Members of the K of P playground degree wore fezzes like their Masonic counterparts and were known as Votaries. The Votaries of the Dramatic Order sponsored the Nomads of Avrudaka for their wives and sisters.

Women related to Pythians could join the Pythian Sisters

who meet in Temples. Today this auxiliary is in better shape than the parent lodge. Young men between fourteen and twenty-one formed the membership of the Junior Order Princes of Syracuse which corresponds to the Masonic DeMolay order. The Pythian Sisters sponsor a group for young girls called the Sunshine Girls.

The Order is confined to the United States and Canada. There are fifty-five grand lodges for the various states and provinces, all subject to the Supreme Lodge which maintains headquarters in Chicago. A few years ago the Knights claimed 3000 lodges but this number has certainly declined.

In its heyday the Order built a chain of twenty-two homes for the aged but some of these have been closed and others have long ago opened their doors to residents who never had any connections with the K of P. Like other fraternities the K of P seeks to offer financial assistance to members in distress.

Officers of a local lodge include the Chancellor Commander, Vice Chancellor, Prelate, Master of the Work, Keeper of Records and Seal, Master of Finance, Master of Exchequer, Master at Arms, Inner Guard, and Outer Guard. The K of P actually published their ritual; the Supreme Lodge declared

> The proper place for the keeping of the rituals is in the castle hall; and it is the duty of the lodge to provide a suitable box or other receptacle, with a sufficient lock, the key of which shall be in the charge and keeping of the Chancellor Commander; and it is his duty to prevent their removal from the castle hall.

The Prelate takes his station opposite the altar. His duties are "to administer the obligations; to offer invocations to the Deity and ask His blessings upon our brotherhood; and to perform all other services required of me by the laws of the order and the by-laws of this lodge."

The Prelate's opening prayer is as follows:

> Supreme ruler of the Universe, we humbly ask thy blessing upon the officers and members of this lodge. Aid us to avoid anger and dissension; help us to work together in the spirit of fraternity; and inspire us to exemplify the friendship of Damon and Pythias. Hear and answer us, we beseech thee. Amen.

No prayers are offered in the name of Jesus Christ or the Trinity.

In the initiation of candidates for the first degree, the rank of Page, the lodge room is prepared by placing an open coffin with a skeleton near the center of the room. Two crossed swords are placed on the coffin and on the swords is the open book of law, the Bible.

The candidates are asked if they believe in a Supreme Being and if they are of sound bodily health. They are also asked, "Are you willing to take upon yourself a solemn obligation to keep forever secret all that you may hear, see or be instructed in — an obligation that will in no way conflict with your creed or your conscience?" On giving the correct answers the candidates are blindfolded and garbed in a white sash.

After the usual lodge instruction and procession around the lodge room the candidate is told to kneel before the open coffin, the blindfold is removed, and he repeats the following obligation:

> I solemnly promise that I will never reveal the password, grip, signs, or any other secret or mystery of this rank, except in a lodge of this order, recognized by, and under the control of the Supreme Lodge Knights of Pythias of the World, or when being examined by the proper officers of a lodge, or by one whom I know to be a member of this rank. . . . [The candidate promises to steer clear of schismatic orders and to obey the laws of the order] . . . To the

faithful observance of this obligation I pledge my sacred word of honor. So help me God — and may He keep me steadfast.

Later the initiate presents a sprig of myrtle to the Vice Chancellor. The Chancellor Commander relates the story of Damon and Pythias for the edification of the new member.

In the second or Esquire degree the candidate repeats another obligation similar to that he gave as an initiate for the Page degree. It includes the statement: "I specially promise that I will not commit to writing any of the secret work of this order, so that it may become known; nor will I permit it to be done by another, if in my power to prevent."

The latter part of the degree includes two endings. The candidate is asked by the Keeper of Records and Seal to fill out a form which asks for his name, age, residence, occupation, and the K of P motto. If the candidate refuses to fill in the blank for the motto and declines the offer of the Keeper of Records and Seal to do so, he is congratulated by the Chancellor Commander and inducted as an Esquire.

Should the candidate fall for the trick and fill in the blank the lodge stages a mock prosecution and the Chancellor Commander reprimands the candidate and reminds him of the obligation he has taken not to reveal such "secrets." He eventually inducts the forgetful candidate as Esquire.

The Esquire preparing for initiation as a Knight carries a shield on his left arm and wears a helmet on his head. The visor is lowered which serves as a blindfold. He becomes an actor in a playlet which forms this third degree.

A group of lodge members take the parts of Senators whose duty is to prevent the unworthy from becoming Knights. At some length they debate the type of test to which the candidate will be subjected. The candidate is led to believe that he must jump barefoot onto a slab of wood holding a number of upright spikes. Naturally the real spikes are removed before he leaps. The final obligation is recited which includes the pledge that the new Knight "will cheerfully and promptly pay all dues and assessments levied by lawful authority." He is then instructed in the remaining signs and grips of the Order.

The Holy Office forbade Roman Catholics to join the Knights of Pythias in 1894. The prohibition also extended to the Odd Fellows and the defunct Sons of Temperance. The instruction to the American hierarchy stated:

> The bishops must endeavor by all means to keep the faithful from joining all and each of the three aforesaid secret societies, and warn the faithful against them, and if, after proper monition, they still determine to be members of these societies, or do not effectually separate themselves from them, they are to be forbidden the reception of the sacraments.

The penalty for joining the Knights of Pythias is not so severe as the automatic excommunication which follows initiation into the Masonic lodge. The Catholic who severs his connection with the K of P may resume full membership in the Church.

In 1896 the Holy Office did allow for nominal membership in the three condemned societies (but not in Masonry) under certain conditions. The Catholic member would give evidence that he had entered the condemned society in good faith. His continued membership would not lead to scandal in his community. He would suffer a grave temporal loss, e.g., of insurance protection, if he left the society. And finally there was no danger of perversion or loss of faith. The Catholic who retained such membership in the Knights of Pythias or Odd Fellows was also cautioned against attending lodge meetings and was asked to send his dues by mail. Under no circumstances was the lodge to be authorized to participate in the funeral service.

Today few Catholics would be tempted to defy the Church by joining as moribund an organization as the Knights of Pythias. Except in a few small communities the K of P lodges have lost almost all prestige and influence. The banality of its ritual, the feuds and jealousies among its top officials, the competition of Freemasonry, and poor leadership have contributed to its rapid decline. Whether Rathbone's invention will see the twenty-first century seems doubtful.

Ku Klux Klan

No secret society in the United States has ever equaled the power and size of the Ku Klux Klan of the 1920's. Nearly 5,000,000 American men belonged to the Invisible Empire in its heyday. Between 1921 and 1925 the Klan seized control of five state legislatures and elected governors in Indiana, Maine, and Colorado.

Because of the Ku Klux Klan, men were murdered and mutilated, friendships broken, political careers wrecked or launched. The Klan's influence was felt from courthouse to state house to the floor of the Democratic national convention. Claiming to protect the values of white Protestant America the KKK eventually turned to terror, intimidation, libel, and murder.

The Ku Klux Klan of the 1920's was the second of three distinct Klan movements. Neither the first nor the third Klans enlisted more than a fraction of the members of the second Klan. All three Klans share common rituals and traditions but there is no historical continuity among them.

Six bored Confederate veterans organized the first Klan

in 1865. Life was dull in the tiny community of Pulaski, Tennessee, and the young bloods missed the excitement of the war. They thought it might be fun to organize a secret night-riding band and little imagined they would be injecting one of the most virulent strains of bigotry into the American bloodstream. One suggestion for a name was the Knights of the Kuklos, the Greek word for circle. Someone saw the alliterative possibilities and came up with the Ku Klux Klan.

The first Klansmen soon discovered that white-robed men galloping around the countryside after dark were able to terrorize the illiterate former slaves. The Klan turned from mischief-making and pranks and became a vigilante organization dedicated to opposing Reconstruction and keeping Negroes in subjection. Other Klaverns of Klansmen sprang up throughout the South. General Nathan Bedford Forrest became Grand Wizard in 1869 and his name gave the secret society a measure of respectability. Albert Pike, second founder of the Masonic Scottish rite, served as a top official of the Klan. This image was tarnished as the Klan waged a war of atrocities against Negroes and federal sympathizers. The KKK's weapons were lynching, tarring and feathering, castration, floggings.

Hoodlums and ne'er-do-wells flocked to don the robes of the Klan. Masked and hidden by the night these men could give vent to their sadism and hatreds in the guise of preserving Southern society. Federal authorities succeeded in persuading Grand Wizard Forrest that the Klan was indeed responsible for the catalog of atrocities committed in the former Confederate states. He agreed to order that the Klan be disbanded in 1869 but not all Klaverns followed his order. A committee of congress investigated the Ku Klux Klan and declared it to be a "fearful conspiracy against society." Congress authorized the use of federal troops to put down the night riding and curb the Klan's vigilante activities. By 1873 the Klan had been stamped out. It had existed for less than a decade and had enrolled only a few hundred thousand members but it was to serve as the model for the far more successful second Klan.

A novel and a motion picture prepared the nation for a revival of the Ku Klux Klan in the twentieth century. The book was *The Clansman* by Thomas Dixon, Jr., a Baptist minister. He wrote his novel in 1905 to show how the Ku Klux Klan had saved the South from a revolution by freed slaves. He portrayed Negroes as barely human creatures and Klansmen as the embodiments of Christian courage and purity.

The motion picture was the *Birth of a Nation* by D. W. Griffith. Again the Klansmen were depicted as saviors of the South during the Reconstruction era. The second founder of the Klan launched his new organization to coincide with the premiere of the film in Atlanta, Georgia.

The man who revived the Klan, William J. Simmons, was born in Alabama in 1880. When he was dismissed from the Methodist ministry in 1912 for moral impairment and inefficiency, he tried his hand at selling and finally became a professional fraternalist. A Mason, Knight Templar, Knight of Pythias, and Odd Fellow, Simmons took a salaried job with the Woodmen of the World.

While convalescing from an automobile accident he concocted a new KKK ritual which he had copyrighted. Just before the *Birth of a Nation* came to Atlanta Simmons invited a group of friends, mostly Freemasons, to join his new society. For their initiation he took them to neighboring Stone Mountain. A petition for a charter for the Knights of the Ku Klux Klan was signed by thirty-four men and granted by the state of Georgia on December 4, 1915.

Recruiting was slow in the early years of the revived Klan. Simmons inserted ads in various Southern newspapers inviting prospective members to join "a classy Order of the Highest Class." By 1919 he had enrolled several thousand second-generation Klansmen.

The turning point came when Imperial Wizard Simmons signed an agreement with a two-man public relations firm called the Southern Publicity Association. E. Y. Clarke and Mrs. Elizabeth Tyler, who ran the association, had previously raised funds for the Salvation Army, YMCA, and Red Cross. The pair was to receive a percentage of the Klectoken (initiation fee) of all new Klansmen.

The two public relations practitioners analyzed the temper of the nation and decided that anti-Catholicism was a more salable commodity than racism. The Klan still opposed Negroes, Jews, Orientals, and aliens but the Roman Catholic Church along with the Jesuits, the Pope, and the Knights of Columbus became the chief targets.

Klan recruiters fanned throughout the nation and did a wholesale business in memberships and white robes. By 1921 hundreds of thousands of citizens in forty-five states had been recruited into the Invisible Empire. Money rolled into Atlanta headquarters and into the pockets of Clarke and Mrs. Tyler. Of the $10 initiation fee $4 went to the Kleagle who recruited the new Klansman, $1 went to the King Kleagle who was sort of a district manager, fifty cents went to the district Grand Goblin, $3 went to the Southern Publicity Association, and $1.50 ended up in the Klan treasury. Robes which cost $1.25 to manufacture were sold for $6.50.

The new Klansman was inducted into the secret society in a lodge room which featured an altar with an American flag, sword, and Bible opened to the twelfth chapter of Romans. After instruction in the principles of the Klan and a prayer the initiates knelt on their right knee and swore the Klan oath. It was given in two parts:

I, ..., in the presence of God and man, solemnly pledge, promise, and swear unconditionally that I will faithfully obey the constitutions and laws and will willingly conform to all regulations, usages, and requirements of the Ku Klux Klan which do now exist or which may be hereafter enacted, and will render at all times loyal respect and steadfast support to the Imperial Authority of same, and will heartily heed all official mandates, decrees, edicts, rulings and instructions of the Imperial Wizard thereof. I will yield prompt response to all summonses, I having knowledge of same, Providence alone preventing.

A little later the recitation of the oath was continued:

I most solemnly swear that I will forever keep sacredly secret the signs, words, grips, and any and all matters and knowledge of the K.K.K. regarding which a most rigid secrecy must be maintained, which may at any time be communicated to me, and will never divulge them nor cause same to be divulged to any person in the whole world. I will die rather than divulge same. So help me God! Amen.

All the top officials of the revived Klan were Masons, most of them also active in the Scottish rite. When Klan recruiters visited a new town they concentrated on the local Masons since they were already presumed to be anti-Catholic and anti-Negro and accustomed to swearing oaths and preserving lodge secrecy. Charles C. Alexander in his book *The Ku Klux Klan in the Southwest* explains:

In fact, the Kleagles commonly began their solicitations in a town by calling on the local Masonic lodge. In 1923 the Klan claimed that 500,000 Masons were citizens of the Invisible Empire. Both Simmons and his successor as Imperial Wizard, Evans, were Masons, and so many Masons joined the Klan that in some communities the Masonic lodge became simply an adjunct of the local Klan unit . . . Some Masons eventually voiced disapproval of the Klan, but Masons were never officially advised not to join the hooded fraternity (pp. 94-95).

A congressional investigation in 1921 seemed to backfire and give the Klan valuable publicity. By 1923 the Invisible Empire counted 2,500,000 citizens and the Klan had become a potent fact of life in the political and social circles of many states in both the South and the North.

In general the Baptists, Methodists, and Disciples of Christ furnished the bulk of the Klan's membership; the Klan found a cool reception among the Presbyterians, Lutherans, Episcopalians, and Congregationalists. Although the Methodist bishops fought the Klan many Methodist ministers served as KKK Kludds (chaplains). Thousands of Protestant ministers not only swore the Klan oaths but helped recruit new members and lauded the Invisible Empire from their pulpits. Many Americans joined the Klan thinking they were engaged in a moral crusade to rid their communities of radicals, adulterers, bootleggers, Catholics, child molesters, Jews, Communists, and foreigners. The vast majority of these Klansmen were soon disillusioned and have lived to regret their action; no one mentions Klan affiliation in *Who's Who* or authorized biographies.

The Klan sponsored a string of newspapers across the country and developed its own peculiar vocabulary. An alien paid his Klectoken to the Klabee (treasurer) in a local Klavern (lodge) and his name was recorded by the Kligrapp (secretary). The Kludd led prayers in the Klavern and assisted the Exalted Cyclops (head of Klan chapter) in following the ritual from the Kloran (ritual book). The Imperial Wizard in Atlanta appointed state Grand Dragons who gathered every two years along with other Klansmen in the Imperial Klonvocation. Meanwhile Klansmen conducted regional business at state conventions known as Kloreroes.

Before long the Klan moguls began to flex their political muscles. The Klan elected its first United States senator in Texas: Earl B. Mayfield. It took over the Republican party in Indiana and swept its candidates into office from the governor's mansion to nearly every city hall. In the Hoosier state almost every second adult male had a Klan robe in his closet. Grand Dragon D. C. Stephenson molded the Indiana KKK into the most powerful Klan organization in the country. Hundreds of thousands of Hoosier Klansmen obeyed his orders and he proclaimed that he was "the law" in the state.

Senator Oscar W. Underwood of Alabama sacrificed his political career by opposing the Ku Klux Klan. Other politicians had no stomach for such sacrifices. For example, Hugo Black joined the Klan in 1923 and remained a member until 1925 when he decided to run for the United States Senate. He received permission to disassociate himself publicly from the Klan so that he could win both Klan and non-Klan votes. Chalmers points out: "Black's resignation from the Klan was a purely political maneuver, so that no embarrassing questions might be raised during the election" (*Hooded Americanism,* p. 314). In 1937 President Franklin D. Roosevelt appointed the former Klansman to the Supreme Court.

Klansmen in Oregon teamed up with Masons and Orangemen to pass a law requiring attendance of all children under sixteen at public schools. The Supreme Court declared this law unconstitutional and upheld the right of parents to choose parochial or private schools for their children.

The Grand Dragon in Oklahoma was the vice-president of the University of Oklahoma, Edwin DeBarr. He held a Ph.D. in chemistry. The University's board of regents reprimanded the vice-president but the Norman chapter of the alumni association issued a statement which declared: "If Dr. DeBarr is a Klansman, then the Klan is to be congratulated on the high type of its membership."

Simmons was unable to keep control of his brainchild.

Dr. Hiram Wesley Evans, a dentist from Dallas who was prominent in Masonic activities, eased Simmons out of his top job in 1923. The former Imperial Wizard received a financial settlement for his interest in the Klan. Evans presided over the rise and fall of the "Empire" until 1939.

At the 1924 Democratic national convention Klansmen succeeded in achieving their two objectives: to block the nomination of Roman Catholic Alfred E. Smith and to emasculate an official condemnation of extremist groups sponsored by Northern liberals. Four years later Klan power had evaporated and Smith won his party's nomination.

Inevitably the opportunists and professional bigots who led the Klan overplayed their hand. Too many hands dipped into the Klan till. Too many crimes were laid at the door of the Invisible Empire.

Grand Dragon Stephenson raped a woman on a railroad train traveling from Indianapolis to Chicago. The victim took poison when Stephenson and his henchmen got off at Hammond and was driven back to Indianapolis and kept prisoner for several days. Lacking medical attention she died several weeks later and Stephenson was charged with her murder. He was convicted of second-degree murder and sentenced to life in the penitentiary at Michigan City. His conviction and the exposure of the moral code of the Indiana Klan leaders signaled the disintegration of the Klan's largest state organization. (Stephenson was paroled from prison in 1950, left the state without authorization, and was captured in Minneapolis. He was returned to prison and released again in 1956. His whereabouts are unknown.)

In 1924 the Klan could muster 40,000 robed members to parade down the streets of the nation's capital while millions of other Klansmen openly paraded down the main streets of other American cities and munched hot dogs at huge Klan rallies. The Stephenson scandal, the exposure of Klan atrocities, and the growing disgust at Klan methods produced a nationwide revulsion. By 1930 Klan membership had fallen below 35,000; the Depression finished off the second Klan as a force in the life of the nation. The Catholic Church purchased the Imperial Palace on Peachtree Street in Atlanta in 1936 as the site for the cathedral rectory. Bishop Gerald O'Hara invited the Imperial Wizard to attend the dedication of the new building. In Kokomo, Indiana, nuns took over operation of the Klan hospital.

A veterinarian, James A. Colescott, succeeded Evans as head of what was practically a paper organization. In 1944 the Federal Government slapped a back tax suit on the KKK for $685,000. The Klan was unable to pay and the state of Georgia revoked its charter.

After World War II an Atlanta obstetrician, Dr. Samuel Green, tried to revive the Klan but he died in 1949. What gave new life to the KKK was the school desegregation decision of 1954 and the other victories of the civil rights movement. Die-hard supporters of the doctrine of white supremacy turned to the Ku Klux Klan but this time there were several competing Klans in the South.

Robert Shelton, a former rubber worker from Tuscaloosa, directs the largest modern Klan, the United Klans of America, Knights of the Ku Klux Klan, Incorporated. Most of his followers live in Alabama, North and South Carolina, Georgia, and Tennessee. Shelton claims to be a Methodist and says his wife is a Sunday School teacher but unlike the 1920's the contemporary Klans can count on slight support from the major Protestant churches in the South. Klan Kludds are likely to be backwoods preachers or itinerant evangelists. James Venable of Atlanta runs the next largest Klan group, the National Knights of the Ku Klux Klan, Incorporated. The various Klan groups probably enlisted fewer than 40,000 members in 1965.

Klan rallies still feature the fiery cross. Klansmen erect a forty- or fifty-foot wooden cross wrapped in oil-soaked burlap. At the end of their evening conclaves the Klansmen ignite the cross and stand in a circle while they sing a hymn such as *The Old Rugged Cross.*

These Klans draw their membership from the frustrated lower class in the South — from men who have little education and few skills, and fear the economic and political advancement of the Negro. If Negroes cannot be kept in an inferior social class they will find themselves at the very bottom rung of the ladder. Klansmen have been indicted for the murder of white and Negro civil rights workers but Southern juries seldom convict a white man of these crimes. Klansmen also attempt to use the boycott and the ballot to intimidate any who oppose them.

Periodically a Klan leader will be quoted in the press as predicting a massive revival of the Klan but his words have a hollow ring. Both major political parties condemn the KKK. Twenty-two states even prohibit the wearing of masks except on Halloween. The mainline Protestant churches join the Catholic and Jewish communities in denouncing the Klan and what it stands for. The FBI has planted informants in many Klaverns and the House Un-American Activities Committee began investigating the various Klan groups in 1965. President Lyndon B. Johnson probably expressed the sentiments of most Americans in 1965 when he branded the Ku Klux Klan "a hooded society of bigots."

Mafia

Practically all the secret organizations described in this handbook are beneficent. Their members try to aid each other and usually sponsor charitable projects for the good of the larger society. The Mafia, on the other hand, is a criminal secret society transplanted to the United States from western Sicily. Its members, the Mafiosi, live by a moral code of their own which contradicts both Christianity and the accepted standards of law and justice.

Pulitzer-prize-winning reporter Ed Reid calls the Mafia "the religion of the criminal classes." The Mafiosi abide by a curious code best summarized as "omerta." This code of omerta not only inculcates an individualistic sense of honor and manliness but imposes a blanket of silence on its adherents. In essence omerta declares: "Talk and you will certainly die; keep quiet and the Mafia will take care of you and your family."

The five chief rules of the Mafia are to render all possible aid to a fellow Mafioso, to swear absolute obedience to the Mafia superior, to avenge an offense against any member as an offense against all, to keep secret the names of Mafiosi and the procedures of the society, and to refrain from ever appealing to the state authorities for redress.

In the United States the Mafiosi built their multibillion-dollar criminal empire on the base of bootlegging during Prohibition. Since repeal they have specialized in the fields of narcotics, extortion, smuggling, gambling, and prostitution. Seeking not only profits but a veneer of respectability the Mafia chiefs have also invaded legitimate businesses including real estate.

Superior organization and loyalty enabled the Mafia to eliminate the Irish and Jewish gangs during the 1920's. Men of various nationalities work for Mafia-operated enterprises but the positions of top authority are invariably held by Italians, usually Sicilians. Known also as the syndicate, the mob, or the Cosa Nostra this federation of criminal bands controls organized crime in the United States. Billions of dollars flow through Mafia hands each year. Mafia-connected families control many of the fruit and produce businesses as well as some tomato paste and olive oil companies.

Some students of the Mafia date its origin as early as 1782 when Sicilians organized to drive the French from their island. One explanation of the term "Mafia" has been that this stands for *"Morte alla Francia Italia anela!"* or "Death to the French is Italy's Cry!" but others deny this derivation.

Entrenched in western Sicily from 1866 on, the Mafia exacted tribute from the wealthy landowners and operated as a second government for many decades. The Mafiosi eventually concentrated on cattle rustling and extortion. Mussolini determined to eliminate the society from Sicilian life and managed to achieve most of his goals by 1927. Employing the ruthlessness of his fascist police and courts Mussolini was able to attack the society in a way which has not been possible for a democratic government. The Allies utilized American Mafia chiefs to make contact with the remnants of the Mafia during the invasion of Sicily and unwittingly aided in the restoration of the society there after World War II.

In the last years of the nineteenth century large numbers of Italians immigrated to the United States. Their numbers included some who lived according to the code of the Mafia. In 1890 the chief of police in New Orleans was murdered and the next year eleven Italian immigrants were lynched by an irate mob; Italy broke relations with the United States over the incident.

Originally the Mafiosi preyed on fellow Italian-Americans by demanding protection money. When the nation introduced the "noble experiment" of Prohibition the Mafia saw the opportunity for huge profits in illegal alcohol. Later they entered the narcotics business. By creating drug addicts they assured themselves of a clientele which would demand their product and pay almost any price. The Mafiosi who control the smuggling and funds needed to finance the narcotics trade remain far removed from the street-corner "pusher" who may be apprehended and convicted.

Most of the major Mafia families are related by marriage as well as nationality. Although their moral code could hardly be more inconsistent with the Gospel many of the Mafiosi are nominal Roman Catholics. Some have received elaborate church funerals but a number of dioceses have now forbidden such displays on the basis that the Mafiosi live by a criminal code and qualify as public sinners. Mafiosi often enjoy the companionship of mistresses, but their wives attend church regularly and their sons and daughters have begun to enroll in universities and to enter legitimate businesses. Some Mafiosi are known in their own communities as benefactors of church and charities.

Whether the traditional initiation is still formally given is uncertain. In this rite the initiate enters a room where the Mafiosi are assembled. On the table in the center of the room is a paper image of a saint. The initiate offers his right hand to two Mafiosi who draw enough blood to moisten the image. The novice takes the oath on the bloody image and then burns it in a candle flame. According to files of the Treasury Department the oath reads:

I pledge my honor to be faithful to the Mafia, like the Mafia is faithful to me. As this saint and a few drops of my blood were burned, so will I give all my blood for the Mafia, when the ashes and my blood will return to their original status.

Millions of ordinary citizens contribute to the coffers of the Mafia. Profits from the factory or office football pool probably end up on the ledgers of the Mafia. Patrons of callgirl rings support the Mafia. Illegal gambling makes a huge contribution to the criminal society.

The Federal Government has launched several investigations of the Mafia since World War II. The Kefauver Crime Commission, which made its investigation in 1951, described the Mafia as "a loose-knit organization specializing in the sale and distribution of narcotics, the conduct of various gambling enterprises, prostitution, and other rackets based on extortion and violence." It further described the secret society as "the binder which ties together the two major criminal syndicates as well as numerous other criminal groups throughout the country."

A low-echelon Mafioso, Joseph Valachi, testified at the later McClellan Committee investigation and disclosed some of the operations of the Cosa Nostra. Valachi has been kept in special custody since his appearance to prevent his assassination.

Most of the study of the Mafia has been undertaken by the Bureau of Narcotics of the Treasury Department. This department is said to have a list of more than 1000 known members of the organization. Agents of Sicilian-American background carry out much of the investigative work since a knowledge of Sicilian customs and dialects is essential.

Of all the damage done to the fabric of American life by the Mafia none has been more unfortunate than the smearing of millions of respectable Italian-Americans by the relatively few Mafiosi. The obvious domination of organized crime by men of one nationality has done incalculable harm to the Italian-American community.

Moose
(Loyal Order of Moose)

Francis Fowler had been a member of the Loyal Order of Moose for six years and had paid about $100 in dues when he was killed in an automobile accident on a lonely highway in Ontario, Canada. His sixteenth child had been born the day before his death.

Since he was a member of the Moose lodge his wife and children were eligible to become citizens of the City of Children, Mooseheart, Illinois. Mrs. Fowler and all but the two oldest children moved to Mooseheart in 1961; someone has estimated that the Fowler family can live at Mooseheart for a total of 143 years.

Mooseheart for the dependents of deceased Moose and Mooschaven, a home for aged members and their wives, are the two best known charitable institutions of the Loyal Order of Moose. The lodge also provides sick benefits and a small death benefit to members.

Open to all "male persons of the Caucasian or White race, who are of good moral character, physically and mentally normal, who shall profess a belief in a Supreme Being," the Loyal Order of Moose now reports slightly more than 1,000,000 members in 3500 lodges. It enrolls members in all fifty states, Guam, Canada, Bermuda, and England.

The Moose lodge was founded in 1888 and by 1893 it had grown to fifteen Watering Places and 1000 Moose. But in a few years membership had slumped to fewer than 250.

The initiation of James J. Davis changed the history of the LOM. Davis was initiated at a national Moose convention in 1906 at which only seven delegates were accredited. He was invited to address the gathering and the enthusiasm of his words prompted the remnant of Moose to appoint him Supreme Organizer on the spot.

During the next two decades David stumped the United States setting up lodges and enrolling members. In 1911 alone he traveled 75,000 miles and spent 300 nights on Pullmans and coaches. By 1928 Davis had brought in 650,000 members in 1709 lodges along with another 59,000 members of the women's auxiliary.

The real founder of the LOM had started life as a poor miner and steelworker. He was always devoted to children and expressed this interest in founding Mooseheart in 1913. Eventually he was invited to become secretary of labor in President Harding's cabinet. Later Davis served as senator from Pennsylvania.

If James J. Davis was indispensable to the growth of the Loyal Order of Moose, the Order was kind to Davis. For years he received a portion of each Moose initiation fee. In 1930 he sold his interest in the LOM to his financial agent and secretary for $600,000. Davis was brought to trial in 1932 when it was disclosed that he had received $173,000 in a Moose lottery which had sold $2,200,000 worth of tickets. After one mistrial he was acquitted.

Today approximately 500 boys and girls as well as a number of widows live at Mooseheart, thirty-five miles west of Chicago. They may remain at Mooseheart until they reach the age of eighteen. The City of Children occupies thirty-nine residence halls and sixty-one other buildings on 1100 acres. The property includes a lake, forty-five-bed hospital, church, skating rink, swimming pool, sports stadium, fieldhouse, and student bank. The Moose provide a kindergarten, grade school, high school, and vocational school to prepare the young people for life.

Both Protestant and Catholic chaplains live at Mooseheart; the children study religion for one period a week in their schools from the third grade up. Two Catholic priests and a number of ministers are numbered among Mooseheart's 6000 former residents.

Davis composed a relatively short (forty-five-minute) initiation ceremony. The governor (top official) of a local lodge asks the sergeant at arms to administer the Moose obligation. He first asks the candidates if they believe in a Supreme Being and whether they are willing to assume the obligation. They then place their left hand over their heart, raise their right hand, and repeat the following obligation:

I, ..., solemnly promise, that I will not in any manner, communicate or disclose or give any information concerning anything I may hereafter hear, see or experience in this lodge or in any other lodge of the Loyal Order of Moose unless it be to one whom I know to be a Loyal Moose in good standing. By this vow I bind myself for all time. Amen.

After the governor welcomes the new members and gives some words of instruction, the lodge performs the Nine O'Clock ceremony. At 9 p.m. all Moose turn toward Mooseheart and pray in silence with folded arms and bowed heads. At the same hour the children of Mooseheart kneel at their bedsides and pray. The governor invites the lodge members to repeat: "Suffer little children to come unto me and forbid them not, for such is the Kingdom of Heaven. God bless Mooseheart."

Next the junior governor addresses the new members and the prelate or chaplain explains the ten "thou shalts" of the LOM. These pertain to patriotism, the home, service to fellowmen, protection of the weak, love of the LOM, tolerance, avoidance of slander of a brother Moose, faithfulness, and humility. The first commandment is "Thou shalt believe in God, and worship Him as thy conscience dictates. Thou shalt be tolerant to let others worship each in his own way."

While the governor grasps the extended hands of the initiates the members sing *Blest Be the Tie That Binds*. The orator says a few words and the governor administers the following obligation:

I, ..., in the presence of Almighty God and those here assembled, do most solemnly promise that I will obey the Laws of the Supreme Lodge of the World — Loyal Order of Moose, and of the lodge of which I am a member as well as all orders of the Supreme Council or of the executive officers of the Supreme Lodge or of the officers of the Lodge of which I am a member.

They also promise to support Mooseheart and Moose-haven, to steer clear of unauthorized Moose organizations, to try to settle any grievances within the Order, to help their fellow Moose. The prelate offers a prayer at the altar. All sing *Friendship We Now Extend*. The governor enjoins the new members to be loyal members.

At the option of the family of a deceased Moose the lodge will conduct a burial service and/or a graveside service. Local lodges are encouraged to observe the first Sunday of May as Memorial Day. The governor asks the sergeant at arms to drape the altar with a black and white cloth. He places a Bible and a flower on the altar and drapes the charter in memory of the dead. The prelate offers a prayer and the members sing *Nearer, My God, to Thee*. The governor presents thoughts on the cycle of birth, death, and resurrection and the prelate offers a final prayer.

Members may elect to receive the second degree which is known as the Mooseheart Legion of the World. There are two higher degrees, the Fellowship and Pilgrim degrees. Female relatives may join the Women of the Moose.

The Lutheran Church-Missouri Synod and the Wisconsin Synod forbid membership in the LOM but the Catholic Church has never objected to this secret society.

National Grange
(Order of the Patrons of Husbandry)

Every night of the week thousands of men, women, and children attend some 600 meetings of the most successful occupational lodge in the United States, the National Grange. Current membership of this lodge exceeds 650,000.

The founder of the Grange, Oliver Hudson Kelley, was asked by President Andrew Johnson to tour the South to see what steps could be taken to rehabilitate the war-devastated rural areas. Kelley, a Freemason himself, proposed that a new secret society dedicated to the advancement of rural life would help serve this purpose.

Along with six companions Kelley founded the National Grange of the Order of the Patrons of Husbandry in Fredonia, New York, in 1867. (The original Fredonia lodge still enrolls 400 members and like all Subordinate Granges meets twice a month.) Taking the Masonic fraternity as his model, Kelley devised an elaborate seven-degree system, but unlike Freemasonry the Grange was opened to both men and women.

Originally only those who tilled the soil were eligible for membership but eventually candidates associated with related agricultural occupations were admitted. Growth was slow in the early years but picked up speed. In 1874 alone almost 6000 new Granges or local lodges were established and membership reached 268,000.

The extent to which nonfarmers infiltrated the Order is demonstrated by the Grange in New York City which consisted of forty-five wholesale merchants and sewing machine manufacturers. As hundreds of thousands of people flocked to join the Grange the officials launched a wide variety of projects such as cooperatives and factories to manufacture farm equipment. When these ventures collapsed because of mismanagement and severe competition membership fell from 860,000 in 1875 to only 124,000 in 1880. The National Grange faced an enormous challenge to regain its role in American rural life.

From the beginning meetings of the Granges were not only ritualistic but educational. Members learned how to become better farmers and how to defend rural interests and make the most of their political power. The National Grange fought for the appointment of a secretary of agriculture in the president's cabinet and when one was appointed in 1889 he was a member of the lodge.

Through the years the Granges have advocated support of the land grant agricultural colleges, establishment of agricultural experiment stations, expansion of rural free delivery. As the percentage of the United States population engaged in farming has declined and as the various state legislatures have been reapportioned the political power of rural areas has eroded. The National Grange has its work cut out to preserve rural influence in American life in the 1960's.

Some 4000 of the 7000 active Subordinate Granges own their own lodge halls which often serve as centers of rural activities. Boys and girls from farm families may enter the Junior Grange when they reach the age of five and remain members of this branch until they become fourteen. The 700 Pomona Granges are district or county associations of Granges. Representatives from the Subordinate and Pomona Granges form the State Granges. In turn delegates from the thirty State Granges comprise the National Grange which occupies an eleven-story headquarters about a block from the White House in Washington, D. C.

Officers of the Subordinate Grange are the master, overseer, lecturer, steward, assistant steward, chaplain, treasurer, secretary, gate keeper, executive committee, ceres, pomona, flora, lady assistant steward. Women may hold any of the offices but the last four are reserved to them.

Membership is open to men and women of good moral character "interested in agriculture and affiliated business" who "have no interests in conflict with the purpose of the Grange." There are no restrictions regarding race or creed.

The Subordinate Grange confers the first four degrees of the lodge. In the first degree the male and female novices typify Laborer and Maid; in the second, Cultivator and Shepherdess; in the third, Harvester and Gleanor; and in the fourth degree, Husband and Matron. The Pomona Grange which meets each month or each quarter confers the fifth or Degree of Pomona. The State Grange works the Degree of Flora and the National Grange works the Degree of Ceres. This seventh degree is conferred once a year at the annual meeting of the National Grange; members of the seventh degree control the secret work of the lodge.

In some respects the Grange resembles a typical secret society. An open Bible rests on the altar in a Grange hall and the American flag is prominently displayed. Some of the symbols and regalia are the pouch, sash, spade, pruning hook, and shepherd's crook.

Only those who have taken the fourth degree are considered full members of the Grange; a man or woman who receives the first degree is known as a provisional member. Minimum initiation fee for the four degrees is set at $3 for men and $1 for women.

In the first degree the candidates pledge their sacred honor that they will never reveal any secrets of the Grange, obey the laws of the state and nation as well as the various bodies of the Grange, show impartiality in proposing and accepting new members, never defraud a brother or sister of the lodge. After they recite the obligation the assistant steward and lady assistant steward remove the blindfolds from the candidate's eyes. The overseer then declares: "My friends, to primeval darkness, covering the face of the deep, came the command, 'Light be.' and light was! and the evening, with its darkness, and the morning, with its light, were the first day." The passage from darkness to light is reminiscent of the first degree of Freemasonry.

As the work of the degree continues the chaplain points out that agriculture is the noblest of all occupations since it was instituted by God in the Garden of Eden. The master of the lodge explains the significance of the tools of this degree: the axe, the plow, the harrow, and the spade.

The second degree continues in much the same pattern of instruction and obligation as the first. A bouquet of roses is placed on the Bible and the master declares: "May the pure teachings of this book mingle with their fragrance, and fill you with the hope that maketh not ashamed, so that no fear shall deter you from doing that which is right." The third degree inculcates the lesson of charity and the fourth degree inculcates fidelity.

The National Grange sponsors a variety of contests such as those in color photography, song writing, and art ("No nudes will be accepted"). Quartets who entered the national competition in 1965 were asked to give their renditions of either *I'll See You in My Dreams* or *Swing Low, Sweet Chariot*.

The National Grange is more deeply involved in political and social questions than most lodges. It publishes an annual statement of its policies and programs which runs to forty-eight pages. In the 1965 statement the Grange supported such measures as "trade with the Soviet Union and other Communist countries, whenever the economic gain of expanded trade clearly outweighs any potential political sacrifice." It approved of the Peace Corps and opposed the admission of Red China to the United Nations at this time. It has always given its blessing to the cooperative movement but it strongly objected to Medicare under Social Security. The Grange asked for "legislation requiring able-bodied persons who apply for or who are receiving relief be dropped from welfare rolls if they refuse to accept employment offered." It objected to any laws "infringing upon the rights of American citizens to bear arms." The proposed amendment to the Constitution to authorize prayers in public schools received no Grange support. And, "The Grange feels that right-to-work laws properly are within the jurisdiction of the state."

Although members of the Grange do not automatically receive life insurance they may purchase such insurance as well as fire, casualty, and automobile insurance from companies owned and operated by the National Grange.

The Roman Catholic Church has never approved or condemned the Grange so Catholics are free to follow their own consciences regarding the secrecy and obligations of this lodge. The Lutheran Church-Missouri Synod considers the National Grange more of a labor union for farmers than a lodge in the usual meaning of the term but it is disturbed by the religious content of the Grange ritual. Members of this denomination have met five times with officials of the National Grange to see if the objectionable features can be eliminated. So far they have met opposition from the Order of Demeter which is in charge of the secret work.

Negro Lodges

Almost every major American lodge — Freemasonry, Odd Fellowship, the Knights of Pythias, the Elks, Moose, and Eagles to name a few — strictly exclude the initiation of Negroes. Some of these orders have even extended the racial ban to Orientals and American Indians. The line of brotherhood has been carefully drawn between the races.

One result of this policy has been the founding of Negro counterparts of many of these white lodges. With relative ease Negroes have obtained the secret rituals of such lodges and set up parallel organizations. Like the Negro Baptist and Methodist churches, the Negro lodges have served as bonds of unity in the colored communities.

Negroes have not overlooked the gap between professions of brotherhood and the systematic exclusion of men and women because of race which characterize so many lodges. *Ebony* magazine commented:

> Like many other chinks in American democracy, Masonry in the U. S. today has not lived entirely up to its creed.

While Prince Hall Masons are undisputedly legitimate by virtue of their original charter, their white brethren have been reluctant to extend a hand of fellowship. This, in spite of their fraternal teachings of brotherly love and the fact that they all pay homage to the biblical black man, King Solomon (p. 28, September, 1958).

White Freemasonry neither recognizes the legitimacy of the Negro Prince Hall lodges nor allows the initiation of men with Negro blood. The exception which proves the rule is an all-Negro lodge, Alpha Lodge No. 116 in Newark, New Jersey, which is under the jurisdiction of the Grand Lodge of New Jersey. Until 1929 Alpha Lodge included both white and Negro Masons but since then it has been a completely Negro lodge. It raises only three or four new members a year. White Freemasons often visit Alpha Lodge out of curiosity.

Reportedly two white lodges in Brooklyn have recently accepted two transfer members from Alpha Lodge; Adelphia Lodge No. 348 in New York City and St. Andrew's Lodge in Boston have each accepted a Negro. The presence of these few Negroes in four out of the nation's 16,000 Masonic lodges hardly indicates a mass movement.

Prince Hall, the founder of Negro Freemasonry, was a mulatto whose father was an Englishman. He and fourteen other Negroes were probably initiated on March 6, 1775, in Military Lodge No. 441 working under the Grand Lodge of Ireland. Prince Hall received a charter from the Grand Lodge of England in 1784 and constituted African Lodge No. 459 in 1787. The 4729 Prince Hall lodges trace their history to this lodge and many Masonic authorities have admitted its legitimacy.

No official recognition, however, has been given to Prince Hall Masonry. The Grand Lodge of New York declared in 1851 that American Indians and Negroes were "unfit" for initiation into the Craft. American Masonry was aroused in 1897 when the Grand Lodge of Washington declared that Freemasonry knew no color line and that this Grand Lodge would recognize African lodges within its jurisdiction. In short order many other grand lodges in the United States and Canada severed fraternal relations with the Grand Lodge of Washington. The complaint was that Washington had given "official recognition" to "clandestine" Freemasonry. Washington bowed to this pressure.

The Grand Lodge of Massachusetts offered partial recognition to Prince Hall Masonry in 1947 but withdrew this recognition two years later when the grand lodges of Florida and Texas severed relations with Massachusetts and California threatened to follow suit. The refusal of white Freemasons to recognize Prince Hall Masons means that no Prince Hall Mason may visit a white lodge. In some jurisdictions a white Mason who even discusses Masonry with a Negro Mason subjects himself to expulsion from his lodge. In Illinois three white Masons once served as pallbearers at the funeral of a Negro Mason. For this crime the white lodge to which they belonged expelled one and suspended the other two white men.

More than 312,000 men belong to Prince Hall lodges in thirty-eight states as well as Canada, Liberia, and Nassau. These lodges form the oldest and wealthiest secret society among United States Negroes. A few Caucasians and Orientals also belong to Prince Hall lodges since Prince Hall Masonry erects no racial barriers. There are also a number of Negro Masonic bodies such as the National Compact Grand Lodge and the John J. Jones Affiliation which receive recognition from neither white Masonry nor Prince Hall.

Negroes have organized counterparts to most of the major white Masonic bodies. Negroes join chapters of Royal Arch, councils of Royal and Select Masters, commanderies of Knights Templar, consistories and supreme councils of the Scottish rite, divided as in white Freemasonry into Northern and Southern jurisdictions.

Negro 32nd-degree Masons and Knights Templar may join the Ancient Egyptian Arabic Order of Nobles of the Mystic Shrine. The 15,000 Negro Shriners meet in 150 Temples and contribute to medical research. They claim their Order was founded by visiting Arab potentates who attended the Chicago World's Fair in 1893. The female auxiliary, the Daughters of Isis, enrolls 6500 women in 117 courts.

Female relatives of Prince Hall Masons may join the Eastern Star. There are also Negro versions of the Grotto and the Tall Cedars of Lebanon.

Outside the United States men of all races are initiated into lodges recognized by the Grand Lodge of England. Even should the state grand lodges reverse their position and allow the admission of Negroes in this country the fact that one blackball can reject a petitioner would serve to keep down the number of Negroes in white lodges.

The Independent Order of Odd Fellows also refuses to admit Negroes. A Negro sailor named Peter Ogden who had been initiated into the Odd Fellows in England discovered that he could not join the lodge in the United States. He received a charter from the Grand Lodge in England and founded the Grand United Order of Odd Fellows which is a predominantly Negro lodge.

A group of Negroes in Richmond applied for a charter for a Knights of Pythias lodge in 1869 but were turned down. They claim that some sympathetic white Knights initiated them into the Pythian secrets but they might also have simply obtained a pirated edition of the ritual. They formed the Knights of Pythias of North and South America, Europe, Asia, and Africa. A smaller group of Negroes founded the Colored Knights of Pythias.

The Benevolent and Protective Order of Elks does not

believe that Negroes should enjoy the benefits of Elkdom but a porter on the Chesapeake and Ohio Railroad seems to have obtained an Elks' ritual. He organized the Improved Benevolent and Protective Order of Elks in Cincinnati in 1898 which has become one of the largest Negro lodges.

Not every Negro lodge is an imitation of a white lodge. The International Order of Twelve or Knights and Daughters of Tabor was established at Independence, Missouri, in 1872; it claims to be a continuation of an antislavery society dating back to 1846. The founders of the Grand United Order of Galilean Fishermen borrowed freely from Scottish rite Masonry when they started their new lodge in 1856. They employ the Masonic symbols of the cross, INRI, and rose. A schism in 1904 gave birth to the Grand United Order of the Fishermen of Galilee of the Eastern and Western Hemispheres.

In no area have the American secret societies shown less courage and democracy than in that of recognizing racial equality. While the public schools, churches, public accommodations, armed forces, and other areas of national life have desegregated, the lodges have held to racial bars. Except for the Knights of Columbus none of the major lodges has welcomed Negro members; their outdated racism has probably repelled college graduates and religious-minded men and women who see no inherent objection to a candidate because of his race.

Odd Fellows
(Independent Order of Odd Fellows)

While eighteenth-century English Freemasonry was attracting members of the aristocracy and mercantile class, less affluent classes began to seek the fellowship and mutual

O

protection offered by the Masonic lodges. These laborers and farmers and mechanics formed "friendly societies" of their own. Their main purpose was to help fellow members find employment when they were out of work.

Historical records indicate that one such society met at the Oakly Arms, Borough of Southwark, as early as 1745. Meeting in various taverns these societies soon won an unenviable reputation for excessive conviviality. One branch in Manchester objected to the drunkenness common in these workingman's lodges and managed to form a federation of like-minded societies in 1812. They adopted a common ritual and soon the Manchester Union claimed the allegiance of most of the Odd Fellows.

The founders of the Manchester Union declared that the main purpose of the Odd Fellows was "to render assistance to every brother who may apply, through sickness, distress, or otherwise, if he be well attached to the Queen and government and faithful to the Order."

This was the start of what is sometimes called "poor man's Masonry" since the Odd Fellows have neither the influence, wealth, numbers, or antiquity of the Masonic lodges. A historical sketch issued by the Independent Order of Odd Fellows admits that the first lodges "were composed of honorable, frugal, humble, and poor laborers with the sole object of providing relief for fellow members in times of distress."

Thomas Wildey, a coach maker by trade and Swedenborgian in religion, introduced Odd Fellowship into the United States. Coming to this country from his native England in 1817, he inserted an advertisement in a Baltimore newspaper inviting any Odd Fellows to get in touch with him. Four Odd Fellows joined Wildey and organized Washington Lodge No. 1 in Baltimore on April 26, 1819. They met in the Seven Star tavern until their boisterousness forced the proprietor to invite them to find another meeting place.

Another Odd Fellow lodge was established in Boston in 1820 and one in Philadelphia in 1821. The American lodges entered a fraternal relationship with the Manchester Union although Wildey had originally belonged to another branch of English Odd Fellowship. This relationship continued until 1842 when the American lodge severed its connection and declared its independence.

One of the reasons for the break with the Manchester Union was that the American Odd Fellows discovered that the English lodge had chartered a lodge for free Negroes in New York. This Negro version, the Grand United Order of Odd Fellows in America, survives but is not recognized by the IOOF.

Growth of the IOOF was hampered by the anti-Masonic agitation following the Morgan affair but by the time Wildey died in 1861 the lodge counted more than 200,000 members. During the Civil War the Sovereign Grand Lodge left vacant the seats of the Southern delegates and remitted their dues and assessments.

Subordinate lodges and the IOOF confer four degrees: Initiatory, Friendship, Love, and Truth; additional degrees were once worked but the four-degree system was stabilized in 1880. Since Freemasons could go on to "higher degrees" the pressure for such additional degrees was felt in Odd Fellowship. This led to the founding of the Encampment Lodge in 1885 which works three additional degrees: the Patriarchal, Golden Rule, and Royal Purple. The lodge calls its parade unit the Patriarchs Militant. The lodge also bestows its highest honorary degree, the Grand Decoration of Chivalry, which corresponds to the Masonic 33rd degree. The IOOF ritual has been revised several times and as recently as 1954.

To offer an opportunity for Odd Fellows to relax in the company of their brothers the lodge organized the Ancient Order of Samaritans as a fun organization. Its councils are headed by the Supreme Monarchos of the Supreme Sanctorums.

The ladies auxiliary of the IOOF, the Rebekah, established in 1851, is open to female relatives and to Odd Fellows. Boys from twelve to eighteen may join the Junior Lodge and girls may enter the Theta Rho Club.

In bygone days the IOOF placed considerable emphasis on sickness and death benefits; the lodge has never provided insurance for its members but has, in effect, passed the hat and voted to allocate funds to members in distress. The workingman who joined the Odd Fellows lived in constant fear that illness or death would put his family into the poorhouse. In recent years the much larger benefits of social security, union and company pension plans, and Medicare have undercut this reason for joining a fraternal benefit society such as the IOOF.

Membership in the IOOF is open to white males twenty-one years of age or older. "Chinese, Polynesians, Indians, half-breeds and mixed bloods" as well as Negroes are specifically excluded. Men engaged in gambling or the liquor business may not apply. At one time the IOOF was running neck and neck with Freemasonry in terms of numbers but the Odd Fellows has been losing members in recent years. In 1934 after several years of Depression the Odd Fellows enrolled 1,623,000 members but today the rolls list fewer than 1,400,000 men; this is less than half the number in American Freemasonry. Of course, many thousands of Odd Fellows also belong to a Masonic lodge. The IOOF has chartered 22,000 lodges in the United States, Canada, Australia, Germany, Switzerland, the Netherlands, Mexico, Cuba, and Sweden.

The IOOF maintains a chain of homes for the aged and orphans which cost $4,500,000 a year to operate and which are valued at $22,000,000. A number of these homes have closed their doors since World War II.

O

Despite its membership decline the IOOF still claims to be the largest fraternal society in the world under one head. The 4,200,000 American Masons give allegiance to fifty state grand lodges rather than to one national grand lodge. The IOOF maintains headquarters in an old mansion in Baltimore, Maryland.

The lodge may initiate a large group of candidates at one time although only one representative of the initiation class goes through the ceremonies; the rest watch.

A candidate for initiation into the first degree is asked seven questions including "Do you believe in the existence of a Supreme, Intelligent Being, the Creator and Preserver of the Universe?" After giving the correct answers he pledges his sacred honor to keep secret whatever transpires during his initiation.

The outside conductor blindfolds the candidate and informs the inside guard that he is accompanying a stranger who wants to join the lodge. The vice grand directs that the candidate be admitted into the lodge room.

Members of the lodge put the blindfolded candidate into chains and form a funeral procession. After marching around the room they take off the blindfold and invite the candidate, who is confronted by a human skeleton illuminated by two torches, to meditate upon death.

Several other lodge officials give instructions and the chaplain offers a prayer. The conductor again blindfolds the candidate and presents him to the warden. The warden asks the candidate to give his age and occupation and asks if he can keep a secret. He asks him to practice friendship and love and truth. Next the vice grand asks him whether he is willing to assume an obligation "which will not conflict with any of those exalted duties you owe to God, your country, your family, or yourself." He is then asked to place his right hand on his left breast and repeat the obligation of the Initiatory Degree:

I, ... , in the presence of the members of the Order here assembled, do solemnly promise that I will never communicate to any one, unless directed to do so by a legal lodge, the signs, tokens or grips, the term, traveling, or other passwords belonging to the Independent Order of Odd Fellows. Nor will I expose or lend any of the books or papers, relating to the records or secret work of the Order, to any person or persons, except to one specially authorized to receive them. That I will never reveal any private business which may be transacted in my presence in this or any other Lodge. I also promise that I will abide by the laws, rules, and regulations of this Lodge, of the Grand Lodge of the Independent Order of Odd Fellows, of (the name of the state) or any other Grand or working Lodge to which I may be attached.

I further promise that I will never wrong a Subordinate or Grand Lodge to the value of anything. Nor will I take part or share, directly or indirectly, in any illegal distribution of the funds or other property of the Lodge; but will, to the best of my ability, endeavor to prevent the same. Nor will I wrong a brother or see him wronged without apprising him of approaching danger, if in my power so to do. Should I be expelled or voluntarily leave the Order, I will consider this promise as binding out of it as in it. To the faithful performance of all which I pledge my sacred honor.

The noble grand welcomes the new member and encourages him to be faithful to the principles of Odd Fellowship. "The moral precepts which govern us, and according to which we would have all men regulate their conduct, are the laws of God. May those laws be indelibly engraven upon your heart, and may they guide and direct your daily walk of life."

The noble grand gives the new Odd Fellow the current passwords and the grip of this degree and explains the procedures needed to enter a lodge. The chaplain and past grand offer words of edification. The latter official explains: "With the divisions and classifications of human society our Order holds no fellowship. While it inculcates a veneration for religion and subordination to civil government and its laws, it studiously avoids all affinity with systems of faith or sects, whether religious or political." After the noble grand imparts the signs of distress and recognition, the Rebekah sign of recognition, etc. the lodge is closed.

In the Degree of Friendship, which is the second degree a new member will take, a lodge may present either a full or an abbreviated version of the work. In the full work the candidate witnesses a playlet based on the friendship between Jonathan and David. In the shorter version the chaplain gives a summary of this playlet. Near the end of this degree the conductor and the candidate kneel on their right knees facing each other; their left knees touch and their right hands are clasped. The conductor intones: "The Lord be between me and thee and between my seed and thy seed, from this day forever." The entire lodge repeats this covenant and the chaplain, vice grand, and past grand declare: "Hail to the covenant of friendship!" The candidate receives further information about the sign, countersign, grip, and token.

The Degree of Brotherly Love, known as the third degree, finds the candidate being blindfolded into the lodge as a traveler going from Jerusalem to Jericho. The conductor leads him several times around the lodge room and finally takes off the blindfold so the candidate can watch a dramatization of the story of the Good Samaritan. Later the noble grand offers further instructions on the secret workings of the lodge and states that the Odd Fellows seek to imitate the example of the Good Samaritan.

In the final or Degree of Truth the chaplain gives a resumé of the preceding three degrees. The various symbols of the degrees are again explained: the all-seeing eye, the three links, the skull and crossbones, the scythe, the bow and and arrow, the quiver, the bundle of sticks, the ax, the heart and hand, the globe, the ark, the serpent, the scales and sword, the Bible, the hourglass, the coffin. The candidate is clothed in the scarlet regalia of this degree, welcomed to full membership, and informed of the "higher degrees" to which the Odd Fellow can aspire.

The Sovereign Grand Lodge issued a statement in 1963 which clarified the relation of the IOOF to religion:

> While Odd Fellowship is not a religious institution, many of its principles, tenets, practices, and objectives are based upon the teachings of the Holy Bible. Many of the rites and ceremonies, much of the ritual and lectures, the secret passwords, signs, and counter-signs, have a Biblical origin or significance. Free and extensive use of the Holy Scriptures is made in much of the secret work of the Order and in the lectures. Recognition of, and subjection to, a supreme intelligent Being as Creator and Preserver and Benefactor of the Universe and of mankind is required of all initiates. Lodges are opened and closed with prayer, and there are special prayers at appropriate stages in the ritual and ceremonies. Reverence for God and for His name, respect and esteem for the Holy Bible, and adherence to the principles of righteousness, justice, and brotherly love in human relations are all inspired and strengthened by the associations and workings of an Odd Fellows Lodge.

Although the Odd Fellows still report well over a million members while many other lodges have all but disappeared, the rate of growth of the IOOF has hardly kept up with the population growth. Young men, especially college graduates, see no great advantages in joining the Odd Fellows unless they are following a family tradition. If they plan to join one fraternal order they are likely to choose the more prestigious Masons. The modest sickness and burial benefits do not impress workingmen covered by social security or union pensions.

Female relatives of Odd Fellows as well as single white women over eighteen and of good character may join the Rebekah lodges. Odd Fellows themselves may also receive the Rebekah degree. The relationship between Rebekah lodge and IOOF is similar to that between the Eastern Star and Masonry. Members of the Odd Fellows and Rebekah lodges jointly sponsor the Theta Rho Girls' Clubs.

Roman Catholics who join the IOOF are denied reception of the sacraments but are not excommunicated. The Catholic Church views the promises of the IOOF as far less destructive to the Christian faith than the oaths and penalties of the Masonic lodges. The philosophy of the Odd Fellows is less blatantly naturalistic than that of Freemasonry and the IOOF has never been a particularly bitter enemy of Roman Catholicism. Catholics may even maintain passive membership in the IOOF under the same condition as those prescribed for affiliation with the Knights of Pythias (see p. 84) who were also condemned by name by the Holy Office in 1894. The antilodge Lutherans and other Protestants ordinarily forbid membership in the Independent Order of Odd Fellows.

Orangemen
(Loyal Orange Association of British America)

Militant anti-Catholicism has animated one of the oldest societies in the English-speaking world since its founding in the late eighteenth century. After a battle between Protestants and Roman Catholics in County Armagh, Ireland, in 1795 a group of Protestants formed the Loyal Orange Lodge to espouse loyalty to the British throne and opposition to Catholicism.

The Orangemen named their new secret society after William III, Prince of Orange, who 105 years before had led the Protestant forces to victory against James II in the battle of the Boyne. The Orange lodges grew rapidly and had initiated 200,000 members by 1797. Northern Ireland wit-

125

O

nessed bloody fighting between Orangemen and Catholics in 1828 and 1829. Finally in 1836 the Orange lodges were dissolved in Ireland but they were revived nine years later.

The Orange lodges were carried to England in 1808; headquarters of the Order was moved from Manchester to London in 1821. In 1827 the Orange lodge, originally a peasant movement, won new prestige when the Duke of Cumberland became Grand Master in England. Army lodges were working in Canada as early as 1812 but the Grand Lodge of British America was not formed until 1830 at Brockville, Ontario.

Eventually the Loyal Orange Institution spread to Australia, New Zealand, and even Africa. When Gladstone declared himself in favor of home rule in Ireland in 1885 the Orange lodges experienced a substantial growth among the Protestant minority.

Orangemen founded the first United States lodge in 1867 and established a grand lodge for this country in 1870. As in Ireland the appearance of the Orangemen provoked rioting and bloodshed. When a band of infuriated Irish Catholics attacked a parade of Orangemen in New York City on July 12, 1871, the ensuing riot cost sixty lives and had to be quelled by troops. During the latter part of the nineteenth century the Orangemen joined forces with the APA and the Junior Order United American Mechanics to demand restriction of immigration to the United States; they objected to a further influx of Roman Catholics.

The official statement of purpose of the Loyal Orange Association of British America is as follows:

> The Loyal Orange Association is formed by persons desirous of supporting to the utmost of their power, the principles and practices of the Christian religion, to maintain the laws and constitution of the country, afford assistance to distressed members of the Association, and otherwise promote such laudable and benevolent purposes as may tend to the

due ordering of religion and Christian charity, and the supremacy of law, order and constitutional freedom.

The lodge works a five-degree system from the first or Orangeman degree to the fifth or Scarlet degree. Scarlet degree members may also apply for membership in the Royal Black Knights of the Camp of Israel. Women relatives may join the Loyal True Blue Association and the Ladies Orange Benevolent Association. Boys between six and sixteen who are the sons of Protestant parents may join the Boys Juvenile Orange Association "uniting them in an organization for education in the principles of Orangeism and Protestantism in general and instilling in them loyalty to the Flag, the English language and the public schools."

An applicant to an Orange lodge must be eighteen, believe in the Trinity, profess the Protestant religion, read the Bible, attend church services regularly, be loyal to the British Crown, and be an exemplary moral citizen. United States members are asked to pledge loyalty to their own government and to the promotion of civil and religious liberty. Obviously not only Roman Catholics and Eastern Orthodox are excluded but so also are Unitarians.

The American lodges take no chances on Roman Catholic infiltration. The membership requirements include a condition that "no person who ever was or is a Roman Catholic, or who shall educate, or cause to be educated, his children or any children in his charge, in any Roman Catholic school, convent, nunnery, or monastery, shall ever be admitted to membership." The legalistic restrictions seem unnecessary since the Loyal Orange lodge holds the same attraction for a Roman Catholic as the KKK does for Martin Luther King.

Orangeism has declined in the United States in recent decades although lodges can be found in Massachusetts, New York, Illinois, Connecticut, Pennsylvania, California, and Delaware. Preuss estimated 32,000 lodge members in this country in 1923 but the membership probably did not exceed a few thousand in 1965. The real strength of the Loyal Orange Association in North America is in Canada where grand lodges operate in all of the provinces. In Canada the Orange lodges couple opposition to Roman Catholicism with opposition to French Canadian aspirations. Toronto is the center of Loyal Orange activity.

In Canada and the United States many members of the Loyal Orange Institution also belong to the Masonic lodge. Masonic influence is evident in the Orange ritual. In the past, presidents of the Association have often been high-ranking Anglican clergymen but this type of lodge obviously appeals only to those Protestants who view the current ecumenical movement with alarm.

Owls
(Order of Owls)

Whatever else may be said about the Owls they do not seem to give a hoot about public relations. Not only were this writer's requests for information ignored but so were letters from the Commission on Fraternal Organizations of the Lutheran Church-Missouri Synod in 1947, 1957, 1960, and 1961.

We do know that the Order of Owls was founded in 1904 by John W. Talbot and some companions in South Bend, Indiana. Its purposes were "To assist each other in business, to help each other in obtaining employment, to assist the widows and orphans of our brothers, to give mutual aid to our brothers in any way that they may need, and assemble for mutual pleasure and entertainment."

A publication of this lodge states "The Order of Owls is a four degree secret society of good fellows, who believe

O

in love, laughter, and the Kingdom of Heaven on earth. It does not believe in postponing one's enjoyments until death." The ritual states: "We advocate no creed. We know there are so many gods, so many creeds, so many paths that wind and wind. We believe that the art of being kind is all this old world needs."

This lodge emphasizes that there are no prayers or other religious features in its ritual. An Owls' publication states: "We have a beautiful ritual but no religious observances. Nothing in the ritual is offensive to any man's religion or irreligion."

The local lodge is known as a "nest." The Owls appoint a chaplain who is known as an "invocator." This lodge has the usual secret ritual, grips, and passwords.

The candidate for membership in the Owls repeats the following obligation:

> I swear in the presence of these Owls that I will abide by and obey all laws and regulations of this order. I will never commit to writing or reveal any of its signs, grips or other secrets, except within the body of duly and regularly constituted and sitting nest of Owls. I further swear I will not cheat, wrong or defraud a nest of Owls or any Owl, or allow the same to be done if within my power to prevent. I will give an Owl due and timely notice of any threatening danger and will if able render assistance.

He also pledges to keep any secrets given to him by a fellow Owl, to protect the sanctity of an Owl's home, and not to join an illegal Owl's organization. He concludes the oath with: "To all this I pledge my sacred word, may God keep me steadfast."

A catechism of the Owls prepared by the founder stated that "Owls do good, speak kindly, shake hands warmly, and respect and honor their women." Talbot was convicted of a morals charge involving a nurse in the Owls' hospital in 1921 and received a sentence of five years in the federal penitentiary in Leavenworth and a $5,000 fine. This was his second offense.

In 1957 the Owls claimed a membership of 202,000 but the current membership probably does not exceed a small fraction of this number. National headquarters is in Hartford, Connecticut.

P.E.O. Sisterhood

For some reason this women's secret society seeks to preserve an unusual degree of secrecy about its activities and ritual. It does not even reveal the significance of its name — P.E.O. — but this is thought to stand for Protect Each Other.

A request for information to the executive secretary of the Supreme Chapter in Des Moines, Iowa, was returned unanswered with the notation that the P.E.O. Sisterhood would prefer not to be included in this handbook at all.

Women over eighteen who believe in God and have lived at their present address for at least a year may petition to join the Sisterhood. It offers no life insurance or other financial benefits. Its main purposes are social and educational and it appeals to Protestant women of some social standing and college education. The 130,000 P.E.O. Sisters support Cottey Junior College in Nevada, Missouri.

The official statement of objectives is as follows:

> To seek growth in charity toward all with whom we associate, and a just comprehension of an adherence to the qualities of Faith, Love, Purity, Justice, and Truth. To seek growth in knowledge and in culture and to obtain all possible wisdom from nature, art, books, study and society, and to radiate all light possible by conversation, by writing and by the right exercise of any talent we possess. To aim at self-control, equipoise and symmetry of character, and temperance in opinion, speech and habits.

R

A chaplain in each chapter is expected "to conduct the devotional exercises at each regular meeting." Meetings open with readings from Scripture and prayers are addressed to "Our dear Father in heaven." A family may request the P.E.O. funeral service for a deceased member; the chaplain, recording secretary, corresponding secretary, and treasurer recite passages from the Old and New Testaments.

Graebner comments:

> In our experience the P.E.O. Sisterhood invests its program with a good deal of snobbery, the object of its propaganda being largely directed to the purpose of making all who are considered eligible for membership feel that an extraordinary distinction is conferred upon them. As a matter of fact, it is an order like any other, with certain cultural or benevolent aims — in this case educational, but intended mainly to satisfy those who have social ambitions (*A Handbook of Organizations,* p. 250).

The Commission on Fraternal Organizations of the Lutheran Church-Missouri Synod has issued a bulletin on the P.E.O. Sisterhood which concludes: "Even though the Sisterhood may have worthy objectives and may be composed of fine, honorable women of the community, the Commission considers it an objectionable society on religious grounds." The Roman Catholic Church has made no statement on membership in the P.E.O. but it would seem to be a society uncongenial to Catholic women.

Rainbow Girls
(Order of Rainbow for Girls)

Girls between thirteen and twenty may join the Order of Rainbow for Girls if they are related to members of the Masonic lodge or Eastern Star. Each of the 1900 local assemblies of the Order must be sponsored by some Masonic or Eastern Star body.

Reverend W. Mark Sexton founded the Order of Rainbow for Girls in 1922 in McAlester, Oklahoma. At the time he was Grand Chaplain of the Grand Lodge of Oklahoma. By 1965 the Order had spread to forty-five states, Canada, Australia, Guam, Japan, Mexico, and the Philippine Islands; it enrolls about 150,000 girls.

Its ritual is based on the ninth chapter of Genesis and on the virtues of faith, hope, and charity. The seven colors of the rainbow symbolize life, religion, nature, immortality, fidelity, patriotism, and virtue. The Rainbow Girls may receive two degrees: the Initiatory and the Grand Cross of Color.

In opening a meeting of an assembly the mother advisor asks all nonmembers to leave who do not belong to the Masonic Lodge or Eastern Star. The choir and officers enter the assembly room and the worthy advisor takes the chair. After presentation of the flag the group recites the pledge of allegiance and sings a stanza of *America*. The credentials of visitors are checked and the worthy advisor welcomes them to the meeting.

Three girls represent faith, hope, and charity. The worthy advisor asks them one by one what their stations represent. Sister Faith explains that her station stands for "an inward acceptance of the Word of God." She explains her place near the altar: "The Altar is the most sacred place in our Assembly Room. Upon it rests the Holy Bible, symbol of white light, from which we derive strength to sustain us through life."

After the other two sisters explain their stations and the chaplain offers a prayer including a blessing for "the great Masonic fraternity," the worthy associate advisor discusses the meaning of the rainbow symbol. She says that it stands for "the ancient promise of God to His people that

He will never again destroy the world." The colors of the rainbow originate in "the great source of the White Light, which is symbolized in our Assembly by the Holy Bible." The Bible is then opened so that "its White Light may penetrate the heart of every member of this Assembly."

In an initiation the candidate and the sister of faith tell the worthy associate advisor that they are traveling to find the pot of gold at the end of the rainbow. The initiate is instructed to kneel before the white altar of promise, press the Bible against her heart, and hold the symbol of the assembly in her left palm. The worthy advisor administers the obligation after the choir sings *Have Thine Own Way, Lord.* Later in the ceremony the candidate is advised to affiliate with some church.

The candidate receives instruction at each of seven stations. At the station of charity she is shown a pot of gold which contains among other things a Bible and a miniature lambskin Masonic apron. The mother advisor asks the new Rainbow Girl to keep a Bible near her bedside each night and open it to the ninth chapter of Genesis.

As a Masonic auxiliary the Order of the Rainbow for Girls is forbidden to Catholic girls. The Lutheran scholar Theodore Graebner comments: "Joining the Rainbow Girls amounts to a deliberate renouncing of the Church in favor of the lodge."

(See **Job's Daughters**)

Red Men
(Improved Order of Red Men)

One of the chief stated purposes of the Improved Order of Red Men is "to perpetuate the beautiful legends and traditions of a vanishing race and to keep alive its customs, ceremonies and philosophies." But should an American Indian seek admission to the Red Men he would be turned down. Only white men may become Red Men. A parallel might be the barring of Irishmen from the Ancient Order of Hibernians or Negroes from the NAACP.

On the basis that it is a continuation of the prerevolutionary Sons of Liberty, the Improved Order of Red Men claims to be the oldest secret society of purely American origin. Actually the Improved Order was founded in Baltimore in 1834. Graebner states: "Its claim of connection with the political secret society of Colonial days can be safely relegated to the domain of fable" (*Handbook of Organizations,* p. 151). Certainly the various patriotic societies such as the Sons of Liberty, the Sons of Saint Tamani, and the various other Red Men lodges adapted features of Indian life into their rituals but the reappearance of such features in the Improved Order of Red Men does not prove direct descent.

A Society of Red Men was founded in Pennsylvania in 1813 but the members soon won a reputation for love of fire water and brought the society into disrepute. Furthermore the Morgan affair which touched off the anti-Masonic agitation made life difficult for most of the secret societies. The new organization founded in Baltimore sought to escape the condemnation by calling itself the "Improved" Order.

Indian nomenclature abounds in the Improved Order. Local tribes meet in wigwams and initiate palefaces into the secrets of the Order upon payment of wampum. Each tribe is headed by a Sachem and the top national officer is the Great Inchonee.

Its government is modeled after that of the Independent Order of Odd Fellows and its degree system is obviously a Masonic derivative. The Hiram Abiff legend becomes the Red Men's third degree in Indian dress.

Membership is limited to white male citizens of the United States twenty-one or over who speak the English language and believe in a Supreme Being. The Order offers the Degree of Hiawatha for boys and the Degree of Anona for girls.

The Degree of Pocahontas is to the Red Men what the Eastern Star is to the Masons and the Rebekahs are to the Odd Fellows. This auxiliary initiates white women over eighteen years of age and of good moral character; Red Men may also take the degree.

Lodge meetings are invariably opened by kindling the council fire and closed by quenching the fire. The chief officers of a tribe are the Prophet, the Sachem, the Senior Sagamore, Junior Sagamore, Chief of Records, Collector of Wampum, and Keeper of Wampum. All documents of the Order are dated from the discovery of America by Columbus in 1492. Months of the year are identified as Cold Moon (January), Snow Moon (February), Worm Moon, Plant Moon, Flower Moon, Hot Moon, Buck Moon, Sturgeon Moon, Corn Moon, Traveling Moon, Beaver Moon, and Hunting Moon.

Three major degrees are worked: the Adoption degree, Warrior's degree, and Chief's degree. There is also a Beneficiary degree for insurance. At the start of every meeting the Sachem declares:

> The primitive Red Men ever recognized a Supreme Being controlling the destiny of their Tribes. No important matter was ever undertaken without an invocation for its guidance and protection. We, as improved Red Men, wisely follow their example and imitate their reverence. Therefore, brothers, you will now rise while our beloved Prophet invokes the Great Spirit in our behalf.

The Prophet then offers an invocation to the "Great Spirit of the Universe." At no time do the Red Men offer prayers in the name of Jesus Christ.

In the playlet of the first or Adoptive degree the members of the lodge enact the role of warriors, braves, and scouts who are out on a hunting expedition. They rest for the evening and a paleface stumbles on their camp. He is captured and condemned by the Indians who take him back to the encampment of their tribe. There the paleface is tied to a stake and threatened with death but the Prophet intervenes and adopts him into the tribe. Each initiate receives the name of some animal, bird, or character trait.

The Pledge of Honor taken by the new member of the Improved Order is administered by the Prophet:

> I, ..., being desirous of becoming acquainted with the mysteries of the Improved Order of Red Men, do hereby solemnly promise and declare, that I will keep secret from all persons, except such as I shall prove to be Improved Red Men, all signs, passwords, and other matters that are to be kept secret.
>
> And I do further promise, that I will never attempt to kindle a council fire unless I am duly and regularly authorized to do so, or assist or participate in any council the fire of which has been kindled by a suspended or expelled brother, or any other person not authorized by the Great Council of the United States to kindle the same.
>
> To all this I promise and pledge my sacred honor, without intending any evasion whatever. So help me the Great Spirit.

The candidate for the second or Warrior's degree is divested of his coat, blindfolded, his head bound in a bandage, and given a bow and arrow. The candidate and his guide are stopped by the Junior Sagamore who cannot tell whether they are friends or foes and asks for a sign of recognition. The Sachem instructs him further in the traditions of the Red Men and gives the candidate a token. Later the Junior Sagamore hands the candidate a bunch of arrows tied in a snake's skin but the guide tells the candidate to spit on them and throw them at the Sagamore's feet. At this the Junior Sagamore screams:

> Warriors, behold! he hurls them from him in
> Contempt. Seize him, and with
> Your clubs beat out his forfeit life.
> First bind him fast, and my faithful knife shall
> Let forth the purple current from his veins
> And drink it quickly up. Seize him, I say,
> And let the unpitying torture rack his limbs.

The candidate is seized by the Indians and tied to a stake. Just as the Junior Sagamore is about to drive his knife into the heart of the hapless candidate he notices the token and drops his weapon. Further instruction in the "mysteries" of the Improved Red Men and the imparting of signs of recognition conclude this second degree.

During the enactment of the third or Chief's degree the Prophet offers a calumet or peace pipe to the candidate and he in turn passes it to the other officers of the lodge who take puffs. The new Chief also receives the sash of this degree, a frontlet for his brow, and a tomahawk on which is engraved an eagle and the letters T.O.T.E. which stand for Totem of the Eagle.

Membership in the Improved Order of Red Men has been declining for several decades. Ferguson reported 515,311 Red Men and Pocahontases in 1935 but today the membership has fallen below 85,000. National headquarters is in Waco, Texas.

Unlike most fraternal orders the Improved Order frankly espouses a particular political and social philosophy, namely conservatism. It opposes both Communism and the welfare state and regularly denounces waste in government. Recently it has been studying the Liberty Amendment to the United States Constitution which would force the government to dispose of more than 700 business-type operations in competition with private enterprise. The supporters of this amendment also ask that three years after its ratification the income tax be repealed as well as the tax on estate and gifts. The Improved Order of Red Men has not yet committed itself to full support of the Liberty Amendment but it seems to favor its adoption.

Rosicrucians
(Ancient Mystical Order Rosae Crucis)

Some secret societies such as Freemasonry impose a strict ban on proselytizing and the Mafia even ridicules the very idea that it exists. At the opposite extreme the Rosicrucians (AMORC) spend more than $500,000 a year seeking recruits through newspaper and magazine advertisements.

These advertisements promise that the Rosicrucians will open the door to success and prosperity and popularity. All the mysteries of life and death, reincarnation, extrasensory perception, and the secrets of the ancient mystical schools will be revealed to those who return the advertisement's coupon to Rosicrucian headquarters in San Jose, California. The advertisements invariably emphasize that the Rosicrucian Order is "Not a Religious Organization."

The hundreds of thousands of men and women who ask for further information receive an attractive booklet entitled *Mastery of Life*. The booklet includes a gallery of distinguished men such as Benjamin Franklin, Isaac Newton, and René Descartes who are identified as Rosicrucians. Elsewhere in AMORC publications we discover that Plato, Jesus, Dante, Aristotle, and even St. Thomas Aquinas were members of this mystical fraternity.

If we were to believe the claims of the California cult,

we would trace the beginnings of the organization to the reign of Pharoah Akhnaton in 1350 B.C. The cult also claims as ancestors the band of colonists who called themselves Rosicrucians and landed in the New World in 1695; they settled in Ephrata, Pennsylvania. By 1801 their settlement had been abandoned. The Order claims other links between itself and various seventeenth-century secret brotherhoods but the historical ties are missing. Actually the AMORC has been around for only about fifty years.

Anyone interested in joining the Rosicrucians will be asked to forward a $5 registration fee to San Jose and to remit $3.50 a month dues. As long as he pays this $42 a year he will receive two monographs a month. The Order asks members to spend sixty to ninety minutes a week studying these lessons, preferably on Thursday night. The dues-paying member also receives the monthly *Rosicrucian Digest* magazine, a membership card, and the password and grips which will enable him to enter a Rosicrucian lodge.

The member may not share his new wisdom with other members of his family or friends unless they too send their dues to headquarters. Members must pledge: "I will keep confidential all reading matter, lessons, and discourses sent to me. . . ."

If an inquirer does not respond to the first mail offer he will later be given an opportunity to become an associate member at only $1.50 a month. The associate member is not entitled to enter a Rosicrucian lodge.

Besides the correspondence courses the AMORC also sells a variety of occult books. One book describes the lost continent of Lemuria and another explains the secret doctrines of Jesus. The founder of the AMORC wrote a book called *A Thousand Years of Yesterdays*. ("It is a story of the soul, and explains in detail how the soul enters the body and how it leaves, where it goes, and when it comes back to the earth again and why.")

People drift in and out of the AMORC but at any one time the membership probably does not exceed 45,000; most of these men and women are studying the cult's teachings by correspondence. Thousands of other Rosicrucians join lodges which meet in secret in their own temples or in rented quarters. These temples and rituals resemble Masonry in some respects although there is no connection whatsoever between Freemasonry and the Rosicrucian Order (AMORC). Both men and women over twenty-one may belong to a Rosicrucian lodge; all must show a paid-up membership card and give the correct password to enter the lodge room.

Such lodges operate in thirty-one states, the District of Columbia, and Puerto Rico. California reports ten of the one hundred regular lodges in the United States with Texas second with eight lodges. Sixteen of these American lodges own the regalia and paraphernalia needed for working the twelve-degree system.

Outside of the United States there are twenty-six Rosicrucian lodges in France, twenty-one in Brazil, eighteen in Nigeria, thirteen each in Canada and Mexico, twelve in England, eleven in Venezuela, eight in Australia. Members of these lodges pay dues to the lodge treasurer who remits a portion to San Jose.

Within the Rosicrucian lodge the Master sits at one end of the chamber on a triangular dias while his counterpart, the Mater, of the lodge sits at the other end. An unmarried girl between eighteen and twenty-one, called the Vestal Virgin, sits in front of the Master and guards the sacred fire which is used to ignite incense. The Shekinah or sacred triangle stands in the center of the lodge room flanked by three candles. The members of the lodge sit along both sides and wear aprons similar to Masonic regalia.

The lodge observes two special feasts: the New Year Feast on or about March 21, at which the fraters and sorors eat a symbolic meal of corn, salt, and grape juice, and the Outdoor Fete held around September 23.

The lodge Master or chaplain performs the Rosicrucian marriage rite which must be scheduled within three days after the civil ceremony. Children of Rosicrucian parents may receive the rite of Appellation if they are under eighteen months; among other things their parents must agree to educate the child in nonsectarian schools. Funeral rites for members of the lodge begin late in the evening in order to finish about midnight. Mourners wear the official purple mourning color and the deceased is dressed in lodge regalia. The body remains in the temple until cremation in the morning.

Rosicrucians are urged to follow certain daily rituals. For example, when the Rosicrucian wakes up in the morning he should face East, inhale and exhale seven deep breaths, and drink a glass of water. Most Rosicrucians become vegetarians.

A student of occultism, H. Spencer Lewis, founded the Rosicrucians (AMORC) in 1915 when he inserted an ad in a New York newspaper. He claimed to have received authorization from Rosicrucian Masters to reestablish the Order in this hemisphere. From New York Lewis moved cult headquarters to San Francisco, to Tampa, and finally to San Jose. He wrote the monographs which are still distributed to dues-paying members. Lewis was accustomed to signing his name with a Ph.D. although he never spent a day in an accredited college or university. When he died in 1939 his son Ralph succeeded him as "Supreme Autocratic Authority" and "Imperator for North, Central, and South America, the British Commonwealth and Empire, France, Switzerland, Sweden and Africa."

In San Jose the cult occupies an entire city block. The Rosicrucian park includes an auditorium, temple, museum, planetarium, art gallery, library, and administration building. Its annual payroll exceeds $650,000. The AMORC belongs to the San Jose Chamber of Commerce.

Lewis drew on the legends of the Rosicrucians which go back to the seventeenth century. Publication of the *Fama Fraternitatis* in 1614 aroused popular interest in the Rosicrucians. This book told of the travels of Christian Rosenkreuz, a fictitious character, who wandered around the Middle East and founded a secret, mystical brotherhood. Since then various groups of astrologers, alchemists, magicians, and cabalists have appropriated the name Rosicrucian.

Reincarnation is one of the basic Rosicrucian beliefs. Lewis explained in his book *Mansions of the Soul:* "We discover in reincarnation and Karma the only rational and acceptable explanation and cause of the seeming injustice of the inequalities of life. . . . The laws of Reincarnation alone make understandable and acceptable the conditions and experiences of our lives." The AMORC borrows freely from Theosophy and incorporates elements of Buddhism, Gnosticism, Cabalism, Masonry, pseudoscience, vegetarianism, and pantheism.

A member who does not belong to a local lodge but receives his instructions by mail is known as a sanctum member. He initiates himself following sealed directions he receives from San Jose and must then relate his initiation experiences in a letter to headquarters. Ordinarily a new member will study six weeks at home before initiating himself into the first degree. He remains in this degree for about twelve weeks before moving on to the second degree. He stays another twelve weeks in this degree before giving himself the third degree.

In the initiation of a sanctum member into the first degree or First Portal the neophyte sets up an altar on which he places a mirror and candles. He darkens the room and reads the instructions which tell him to light the candles. On lighting the first candle he says: "Blessed Light,

Symbol of the Greater Light, cast thy rays in the midst of darkness and illuminate my path."

The candidate sits down before the altar and whispers: "Before I may cross the Threshold I must face the terrors of my life. The Terror of the Threshold awaits me and I need now the strength of the Divine within me." He traces the sign of the cross on the mirror and says, "Hail, O Sacred Symbol of Life, Love, and Resurrection. In the center of thy holy body shall come the Rose, the Soul of man's being, and thou shalt be my sign! Hail, Rosy Cross!" He stares at the cross for three minutes.

He now answers a series of nine questions posed in the instructions and repeats several meditations. He extinguishes one candle and moves the other closer to the mirror. He peers into the mirror and declares: "Reveal, O soul of me, thyself as I have made thyself in the eyes of the Cosmic!" He meditates for another five minutes, puts out the second candle, and exclaims: "Into physical darkness do I walk and move and have material expression, but the Greater Light dwelleth now within." He is now initiated into the first degree.

He makes his reports for Rosicrucian headquarters and signs the Great Oath which binds him to keep secret the ritual of the Order, to live a clean life, to obey the AMORC authorities, and to be a good citizen.

For the second degree the candidate cuts out a white cardboard triangle. At two ends of the triangle he sets candles and in the center a dish with a cube of incense. He ignites the candles and the incense. Making the sign of supplication by crossing his arms and touching his shoulders with his hands he asks his absent Masters for guidance during his initiation. The rest of the rite consists mainly of prayers and invocations.

In the third degree the initiate faces East, pronounces an invocation, holds his hand over his heart, and prays that he may replace hatred with love. He takes three deep breaths and reads:

> The Divine essence which I breathe into my body brings with it an influx of the Soul of God; and I likewise breathe out of my body the exhausted essence which has given me life and maintained the Soul in my body. All evil influence surrounding my soul and contaminating my body went forth from my body with the passing of the exhausted and devitalized breath. With the newer breath, the sweet and holy air, I took into my body the purer essence, which is Divine and is God.

He next raises his hand and pronounces the sounds "Oo . . . ah . . . ee . . ." three times. After five minutes of further meditation he repeats the sounds. This utterance is supposed to "attune the Soul vibrations for purification."

In the second part of this degree the candidate again sets up the altar, candles, and mirror. He is instructed to repeat "Ra, Ra, selah, Ra" which will summon the herald of the Master. He is told how to call upon the guardian by putting the left palm over his heart and tilting his head back. He engages in a make-believe dialogue with the guardian, extinguishes the lights, and sits in the darkness for ten minutes while concentrating on the great Cosmic Temple. He copies down the oath:

> I shall strive forever to deserve the approbation of all good Souls on earth and to serve God silently and peacefully, not in fear of the future made, but in consideration of an unmade future, a realm for my greater development. So mote it be.

After writing each seventh word he is directed to stop, look into the mirror and repeat this word seven times.

The third part of this degree calls for the same preparations. The initiate gazes into the mirror and repeats "O Worshipful Master of the Divine powers on earth, attune my soul with the Cosmic and bring the greater light to my mind, as I sit in this silent chamber and await thine orders." He is told to stand up, close his eyes, put his hands at his side and experience the terror of the threshold for two minutes. He reads the password for this degree: "Moard-Moarc." He is to sit and stare at the mirror for another ten minutes and end with "So mote it be."

The third degree member can still proceed to the nine Temple degrees. A Rosicrucian elite forms the Illuminati who have received all the degrees and distinguished themselves in the service of the cult.

The AMORC does not have the Rosicrucian field to itself. There are at least three rival Rosicrucian groups in the United States: the Rosicrucian Fellowship in Oceanside, California, the Rosicrucian Brotherhood of Quakertown, Pennsylvania, and the Society of Rosicrucians, Incorporated, of New York City. Mrs. Nesta Webster comments:

> . . . nothing is easier than for anyone to make a compound out of Jewish Cabalism and Eastern theosophy and to label it Rosicrucianism; but no proof whatever exists of any affiliation between the self-styled Rosicrucians of today and the 17th century "Brothers of the Rosy Cross" (*Secret Societies and Subversive Movements,* p. 96).

In his 649-page history of Rosicrucianism entitled *The Brotherhood of the Rosy Cross* A. E. Waite mentions the AMORC and other modern Rosicrucian bodies but dismisses them with: "They represent individual enterprises which have no roots in the past."

Canon lawyers agree that the publications of the Rosicrucians (AMORC) fall under the ban of Canon 1399 which forbids books which favor superstition or subvert the Christian religion. The whole AMORC system — reincarnation, Karma, pantheism, etc. — stands in opposition to Christianity. The solemn oaths which are essential in the Rosicrucian degrees would be considered as objectionable by the Catholic Church as the Masonic oaths.

Royal Arcanum

The arcanum of the Royal Arcanum seems to be how to buy insurance at lower rates than those offered by commercial insurance companies. This fraternal benefit society was founded in 1877 in Boston by Darius Wilson. He was also a member of the Ancient Order of United Workmen and other fraternal societies and had founded the Knights of Honor.

Wilson wanted to refine some of the insurance features of the Knights of Honor. Most of the early fraternal benefit societies accepted members without medical examination and assessed the same rates for men of twenty-one as for those in middle age. Wilson wanted to scale assessments according to age and risk but his Knights did not accept his proposal. He withdrew and founded the Royal Arcanum.

The new society enjoyed rapid growth so that by 1905 it enrolled 316,000 members but many of these were beyond fifty years of age. Some restrictions were placed on membership and the total today is about 55,000. The Order is open to white males between sixteen and sixty who believe in a Supreme Being and are in good health.

The Royal Arcanum works an elaborate ritual which has been twice revised. The number 1105 and the Order's motto — Mercy, Virtue, and Charity — have mystical significance known only to the initiates. Candidates take the following obligation:

> In the presence of the Almighty God and these witnesses I do, of my own free will and accord, most solemnly promise that I will strictly comply with all laws, rules and usages of this fraternity, established by the Supreme Council of the Royal Arcanum. I will hold allegiance to said Supreme Council and be loyal thereto as the supreme authority of the entire Order. I will obey all orders emanating from the Supreme Council or Grand Councils, or from the Subordinate

Council of which I am a member, so long as they do not conflict with my civil or religious liberty. I will not defraud or wrong any department of this Order or any member thereof, or suffer it to be done by others if in my power to prevent. I will never introduce anything of a political or sectarian character at any meeting of, or in any way bring reproach upon, this Order. I will forever keep secret all that may transpire during my initiation and will never improperly communicate to any person any of the words, signs, or tokens; and should I be expelled from, or leave, the Order, I will consider this obligation as binding out of it as in it. I will assist a distressed brother or his family when in distress, as far as it is in my power, without material injury to myself and family. I will answer all proper signs of the fraternity and use all proper means to protect a brother from defamation. And should I violate this my solemn promise, I hereby consent to be expelled from this fraternity; and may God aid me to keep and perform all of these obligations!

The emblem is a royal crown encircled by ten Maltese crosses. The Order maintains its headquarters in Boston, Massachusetts.

Royal Neighbors

Basically the Royal Neighbors is an auxiliary of the Modern Woodmen of America. Membership is open to Woodmen and their female relatives. Founded in 1892, it was reorganized in 1895 as a separate benefit society.

The Royal Neighbors conduct a secret initiation and include an altar, Bible readings and prayers, and a chaplain, called the Worthy Chancellor, in their initiations and meetings. The Order admits qualified white men and women between the ages of sixteen and sixty. The Order is headed by a Supreme Oracle.

(See **Woodmen**)

Sciots
(Ancient Egyptian Order of Sciots)

A group of Master Masons in San Francisco founded the Boosters club in 1905 which became the Ancient Egyptian Order of Sciots in 1910. Limited to California and Arizona this Order functions as a social organization for Master Masons much as do the Grotto and Tall Cedars of Lebanon.

Each Sciot promises to visit his own Blue Lodge at least once a month. The ritual is supposedly based on events which took place on the island of Sciot off the coast of Syria in 1124 B.C. A Toparch presides over local chapters known as Pyramids. The Sciots have fostered public school week which is sponsored by the Grand Lodge of California.

Shrine
(Ancient Arabic Order of Nobles of the Mystic Shrine)

Many people seem to think that the Ancient Arabic Order of Nobles of the Mystic Shrine confers a Masonic degree, in fact, one of the highest Masonic degrees. It does not. Strictly speaking it is not even a part of Freemasonry.

Although the Shrine limits membership to Masons who have achieved the 32nd degree of the Scottish rite or the Knights Templar degree of the York rite, it is not a part of the Masonic system and its burlesque ritual has nothing to do with Freemasonry. As a matter of fact the Grand Lodge of England, the mother lodge of world Masonry, threatens with expulsion any English Mason who enters the Shrine. English Freemasonry considers the Shrine vulgar and banal. No United States grand lodge accords any official

S

recognition of the existence of the A.A.O.N.M.S. although
they do not publicly offer objections to membership.

The teetotaling atmosphere of American Masonic lodges
helped create the conditions which gave birth to the Shrine.
Unlike their English and continental counterparts, the
American lodges have traditionally been "dry." Even the
historical Masonic toasts cannot be offered with anything
more than ginger ale at an American lodge banquet. But not
every American Mason shared the total abstinence position.
A group of thirteen Masons who had been meeting for
weekly luncheons in New York City set about to organize
a fun and drinking society in 1870. This was the start of
the Ancient Arabic Order of Nobles of the Mystic Shrine.

Two men, a physician and a stage comedian, spear-
headed the organization. Dr. Walter M. Fleming concocted
the Shrine ritual which offers a caricature of the Moslem
religion for the amusement of American Masons. Of course,
he attributed his creation to ancient sources and claimed
that the new Masonic playground was really the western
hemispheric branch of an Arabic vigilante association; it
was said to have been founded in A.D. 644 by Mohammed's
son-in-law, Kalif Alee. To attract a better class of members
the founders stipulated that the Nobles belong to the 32nd
degree or the Knights Templar. They had no intention to
establish a new degree within Freemasonry.

Billy Florence, the Jack Benny of his day, was the other
chief founder. He was born William J. Conlin, the son of
Irish immigrants. Although baptized and raised a Catholic
he joined a Masonic lodge in Philadelphia in 1853 and remained an indifferent Mason, save for two suspensions for
nonpayment of dues, until his deathbed. With only hours to
live he renounced Freemasonry, received absolution and the
last rites of the Church. Billy Florence was buried in 1891
from St. Agnes Church at 43rd off Lexington in New York
City. His pastor told a *New York Sun* reporter: "Mr.

Florence was a good Catholic at heart . . . Billy Florence was a noble man, and I am sure that when he became a Mason he did not do so with the idea of being contrary to his Church." The Grand Lodge of New York forbade any Masonic honors at his funeral because of his renunciation of the lodge but the Shrine which he and Dr. Fleming founded sent a floral piece in the form of a square and compasses.

Dr. Fleming was later divorced by his wife and dropped out of active participation in the Shrine. He died practically penniless in 1913 and members of his family complained that he had squandered a small fortune in the pursuit of Masonic degrees and honors.

By 1878 the Shrine enrolled 425 Nobles in thirteen Temples. Those who "crossed the burning sands" to join the Shrine usually did so to quench their thirst on "camel's milk."

After fifty years of fun, games, and "camel's milk" the Shrine had won an unenviable reputation for itself. Some grand lodges such as that in Oregon debated whether to expel any Masons who entered the Shrine. The fun organization was giving Masonry a bad image.

Some Shriners also expressed concern over the low opinion most people held about the Shrine and at the 1920 convention they proposed that the organization undertake some humanitarian project to justify its existence. Someone suggested that the A.A.O.N.M.S. establish one or more hospitals to care for crippled children. A Shrine hospital would be open to all crippled children under fourteen whose parents were unable to pay for proper medical care; the children would be accepted without regard to race or creed. Each Shriner would pay a $2 a year assessment to finance the project.

Envy of the Catholic network of hospitals was one of the chief factors in urging approval of the hospital project.

Some Nobles worried lest Negroes and Catholics benefit from Masonic charity but eventually the proposal was adopted. Sam P. Cochran, a Christian Scientist from Dallas, became chairman of the hospital committee and served in this capacity for twenty-four years.

Today the Shrine supports a chain of seventeen orthopedic hospitals including two in Canada and one in Mexico. The Order plans to open three more for the treatment of serious burns in the near future. Not only has the Shrine helped an estimated 250,000 boys and girls but it rehabilitated its own reputation. No one cares to criticize an organization which helps crippled children.

To pay for the operation of these institutions the Shrine now assesses its members $5 a year. It also gets funds from Shrine circuses, the East-West Shrine game, and from gifts and bequests. It costs about $6,000,000 a year to run the hospitals.

Warren G. Harding became the first president of the United States to wear the red Shriner's fez and he would be followed by Presidents Roosevelt and Truman. Today membership in the A.A.O.N.M.S. exceeds 825,000 which means that one American Mason out of five belongs to a Shrine Temple.

An eligibile Mason pays an initiation fee of $100 to $150 to enter the Shrine. He must also maintain membership in his Blue Lodge and in the higher rite, Scottish or York, to which he belongs. The Shrine also levies assessments and annual dues and often calls for expenditures for fez, lapel pins, costumes, banquets, and social affairs.

Shriners support 160 Temples in North America. A few of these count thousands of Nobles and one in Los Angeles records 22,000 members. Initiation classes often exceed 300 men. Local officers carry such grandiose titles as the Most Illustrious Grand Potentate, the Illustrious Grand Chief Rabban, and the Illustrious Grand High Priest and

Prophet. Temples sponsor drill teams, glee clubs, bands, camel brigades, horse patrols, etc.

One Imperial Potentate of the Shrine characterized the spirit of the A.A.O.N.M.S. when he said: "Little boys play cops and robbers; Shriners play Moslems and infidels."

The furnishing of the lodge room of the Shrine includes a canopy or tent in a cart, a pedestal which supports a gavel and scimitar, the Altar of Obligation on which rests the Bible and the Koran, the one-foot-square Black Stone or Holy Stone, two crossed swords, the Altar of Incense, a bier and coffin.

Inside the Temple after preliminary remarks the High Priest greets the initiates:

> By the existence of Allah and the creed of Mohammed, by the legendary sanctity of our Tabernacle at Mecca, we greet you, and in commemoration of the Arab's faith in purity and innocence, we accept your answers as sincere, and you will now be permitted to proceed in the rites and ceremonies of the Mystic Altar of Obligation.

The new Nobles now take the following oath:

> . . . , of my voluntary desire, uninfluenced and of free accord do hereby assume, without reserve, the Obligations of the Nobility of the Mystic Shrine, as did the elect of the Temple of Mecca, the Moslem and the Mohammedan. I do hereby, upon this Bible, and on the mysterious legend of the Koran, and its dedication to the Mohammedan faith, promise and swear and vow on the faith and honor of an upright man, come weal or woe, adversity or success, that I will never reveal any secret part or portion whatsoever of the ceremonies I have already received, that are about to be communicated to me and that I may hereafter be instructed in, to any person in the world, except he be known to be a well-known member of the Order of Nobles of the Mystic Shrine, and I, knowing to an absolute certainty that he or they may be truly and lawfully such, and of good standing with such Nobility. That I will not be present, aid or countenance the conferring of the Order of the Mystic Shrine

upon any person who is not a Masonic Knight Templar or a 32nd degree A. and A. Scottish Rite Mason in good standing.

I further promise and vow that I will not willfully write, cut, speak or portray any detail that might be construed into even a clue to the same, except for official Temple work.

Furthermore, I do here register a sacred vow, promising should I live to become a member, I will impartially cast a black ballot without fear or favor against friend or foe applying for membership in the Nobility of the Mystic Shrine, whom I believe to be disgraced, dishonored, a thief, a perjurer, a murderer, a lunatic, an idiot or a criminal. And should I undismayed pass safely through the Moslem test and be found worthy of the confidence of my fellows albeit I do not actively espouse the cause, still I do promise to be silent, even if neutral, and not oppose the purposes of the order.

I further promise and vow that I will obey the laws and submit to the decrees of the Parent Temple, the Imperial Grand Council of the United States of America, and that I will not acknowledge, recognize nor be present in any other body of Nobles of the Mystic Shrine, claiming to be superior in authority, nor be present in any clandestine Temple not holding constitutional authority from the Imperial Grand Council of the Mystic Shrine.

I furthermore promise and vow that to the full measure of my ability I will never swerve from justice nor duty. That I will respect virtue; protect the innocent; assist the distressed; promote the inculcation of honor and integrity and dispense reasonable charity. That I will protect and defend the unsullied honor of any Noble of the Mystic Shrine, when absent, if assailed; and now upon this sacred book, by the sincerity of a Moslem's oath I here register this irrevocable vow, subscribing myself bound thereto as well as binding myself by the obligation of the prerequisite to this membership, that of a Knight Templar or that of a 32nd degree A. and A. Scottish Rite Mason. In willful violation whereof may I incur the fearful penalty of having my eyeballs pierced to the center with a three-edged blade, my feet flayed and I be forced to walk the hot sands upon the sterile shores of the Red Sea until the flaming sun shall strike me with a livid plague, and may Allah, the god of Arab Moslem and

Mohammedan, the god of our fathers, support me to the entire fulfillment of the same. Amen. Amen. Amen.

At the conclusion of this oath the prospective Nobles are asked to kiss the Christian Bible. The initiation continues as the Nobles engage in various pranks and ritualistic shenanigans.

Some well-known Americans who have joined the Shrine include Harold Lloyd (a former Imperial Potentate), Thomas E. Dewey, Barry Goldwater, Red Skelton, Irving Berlin, Arthur Godfrey, and Chief Justice Earl Warren. Incredible as it appears to English Freemasons some Protestant ministers and even a scattering of bishops have sworn the Shriner's oaths on the "faith of a Moslem."

A party of Shriners sailing to Hawaii in 1911 got the idea of an even more exclusive group drawn from the membership of the Shrine. They called their organization the Royal Order of Jesters and accepted Nobles on invitation only. "Mirth is king" has become the Jesters' motto. Each court of Jesters is allowed to initiate only thirteen new members a year; each pays an initiation fee of $33.13.

Coil, the Masonic encyclopedist, calls the Jesters the "funnier of the funniest" and adds: "This exclusiveness naturally made the Order a coveted honor, though the obvious miscalculation is that those prominent enough and aristocratic enough to deserve so much honor would not always, if ever, be those endowed with unlimited and spontaneous wit and frivolity" (*Coil's Masonic Encyclopedia,* p. 199). The Royal Order of Jesters reports about 20,000 members or one Jester to forty Nobles.

Wives and other female relatives of Shriners organized the Daughters of the Nile in 1913. Another Shrine auxiliary is the Ladies' Oriental Shrine of North America.

Since Negroes could not qualify for membership in the A.A.O.N.M.S. they set up their own Ancient Egyptian Arabic Order of the Nobles of the Mystic Shrine for North and South America. They use a pirated ritual identical to that worked by the white Shriners.

(See **Freemasonry, Grotto, Negro Lodges, Tall Cedars of Lebanon**)

Sons and Daughters of Liberty

White, native-born Protestants between the ages of fifteen and forty-five may join the Sons and Daughters of Liberty. Founded in 1877 as the Daughters of Liberty, this patriotic fraternal benefit society changed its name to the Sons and Daughters of Liberty in 1915. It began as an adjunct of the United American Mechanics.

The objects of the Order are to "maintain and preserve the sacredness of the Sabbath," "to maintain, preserve, and protect the public school system," and to instill patriotism and love of country in the hearts of children. The Sons and Daughters of Liberty believe that the Bible should be read in all public schools and the American flag displayed in every classroom.

Historically this organization has displayed an anti-Catholic bias and an opposition to immigration to the United States. It claimed over 100,000 members in the 1920's but has shrunk to a fraction of this total. The headquarters is in Philadelphia.

Tall Cedars of Lebanon

Similar to the Grotto but limited to about a dozen states, the Tall Cedars of Lebanon serves as a fun organization for Master Masons. This Order started in Trenton, New Jersey, in 1902 and the first nine Forests were chartered in Trenton. Most of the 100 active Forests operate in New Jersey, Pennsylvania, and Washington, D. C. The Tall Cedars confers the two degrees of the Royal Court and the Sidonian and enrolls about 50,000 members.

(See **Grotto**)

True Sisters
(United Order True Sisters, Inc.)

More than 12,000 Jewish women belong to the United Order True Sisters, Inc., which claims to be the oldest national women's fraternal organization. It was founded in New York City on April 12, 1846, by a group of women dedicated to fraternalism and to humanitarian causes.

The national philanthropy of the True Sisters is the U.O.T.S., Inc., Cancer Service. They expend about $100,-000 a year on the treatment, care, and rehabilitation of cancer patients. Local lodges spend another $600,000 on projects in their communities such as Jewish charities, scholarships, hospitals, summer camps, refugees, and youth work.

Although the initiation is closed to nonmembers the True Sisters do not require an oath. The organization does not offer any insurance benefits.

Order of United Commercial Travelers
of America

To the best of our knowledge the farmers' daughters of the nation have not yet formed a protective sorority but the traveling salesmen can join the Order of the United Commercial Travelers of America. To date almost 300,000 such salesmen have joined the 667 councils of this secret occupational fraternity. One of the Order's goals is "to secure just and equitable consideration for all salesmen, businessmen, and professional men."

This Order was founded in Columbus, Ohio, in 1890. It seeks to unite traveling salesmen who are white male citizens of the United States, Canada, or the British possessions in North America who possess good character and good health. No one under eighteen or over fifty-five years of age is eligible for insurance membership. Those ineligible for insurance may become associate members.

The United Commercial Travelers of America pays accident, sickness, and death benefits. A new member can receive insurance protection by simply signing the application but most members go through the secret initiation. The preparatory obligation reads: "I, ..., solemnly obligate myself to assist the dependent widows and orphans of my deceased brethren, observe and obey the laws of my country, aid in caring for the sick and burying the dead."

Later in the initiation ceremony the candidate puts his left hand on the Bible and repeats: "I, ..., promise upon the faith of an honest man never to reveal the secrets of this Order, nor the nature of any business transacted in my presence within these walls, to any person or persons in the world, unless I shall be morally certain that he or they are as justly entitled to the same as I am myself." He then promises to obey the laws of the Order, to aid brother commercial travelers and defend their honor, to advance the interests of the Order, to defend the character of woman, and never to violate the chastity of a maiden. The oath concludes: "To all of this I most solemnly and sincerely promise and swear, with a firm and steadfast purpose to perform the same, invoking the aid of Him who holdeth the seas in the hollow of His hands to keep me faithful and true. Amen."

A chaplain conducts devotional exercises at the opening and closing of meetings of the lodge. Members observe the Sunday nearest April 9 as Memorial Day for United Commercial Travelers who have made their last sale.

White Shrine of Jerusalem

Master Masons and their wives, mothers, daughters, widows, and sisters may apply for membership in the White Shrine of Jerusalem if they profess "a belief in the defense of the Christian religion." This and the ritual which is based on the birth and life of Christ eliminate Jewish Freemasons and their female relatives from this Order.

For many decades the White Shrine sought to serve as a social organization for Christian members of the Order of the Eastern Star. But the OES consistently refused to recognize the White Shrine in any way as it has also refused to acknowledge the Order of Amaranth. In 1953 the White Shrine modified its requirements, which had required Eastern Star membership as a prerequisite; it opened its doors to any Master Masons and their female relatives. Since that decision the White Shrine of Jerusalem has gained members and now counts more than 180,000 Sojourners in some 800 Shrines.

Charles D. Magee founded the White Shrine of Jerusalem in Chicago on October 23, 1894, but three years later he withdrew from the original body and set up a rival White Shrine in Grand Rapids, Michigan. Each unit sought similar objectives but each worked a slightly different ritual and chartered its own subordinate lodges.

Finally in 1909 the two Supreme Shrines settled their differences and got together as the Supreme Shrine of the Order of the White Shrine of Jerusalem as organized under

the laws of the state of Illinois. It has grown throughout the
United States and Canada. The presiding officer is known
as the Supreme Worthy High Priestess.

The Eastern Star still insists that the White Shrine is no
part of the OES system and is in no sense a higher degree
of the Eastern Star. Apparently the Eastern Star wanted to
avoid the bane of the Masonic Blue Lodge — the member who joins and continues to pay dues only to maintain
membership in a higher rite such as the Scottish or the
Mystic Shrine.

The White Shrine seeks to offer a more Christian atmosphere than the deistic one of the Eastern Star. Its ritual
prayers are frankly offered in the name of Jesus. For example in its memorial service a Sojourner taking the part
of the Angel Gabriel declares: "Henceforth, and for all
eternity, they shall be Sojourners of our Supreme Immortal
White Shrine in the New Jerusalem and privileged to meet
Our Savior 'Face to Face.' "

(See **Eastern Star**)

Woodmen
(Modern Woodmen of America)

Joseph Cullen Root of Lyons, Iowa, invented the Modern
Woodmen of the World which is primarily an insurance
society with certain lodge features. He had long devoted
his energies to fraternalism as a Mason, Knight of Pythias,
Odd Fellow, United Workman, and Chief Rector of a secret
society known as the V.A.S.

Root, who was a small businessman and a lawyer, had
once written a play entitled "Consolidation" and hankered
to try his hand at a lodge ritual. Drawing on elements of
ritualism from the many lodges to which he belonged Root

concocted a four-degree system with scenes set in a forest and a Roman court. When he happened to hear a sermon about a man clearing a forest he hit upon a name for his new lodge: the Modern Woodmen of America. He intended to found an order which would bind "Jew and Gentile, the Catholic and Protestant, the agnostic and atheist."

The first Camp of the Modern Woodmen of America was founded in 1883. At first Root limited solicitation of members to the twelve "healthiest" states of the union: Illinois, Minnesota, Iowa, Nebraska, Wisconsin, Michigan, Kansas, North and South Dakota, Missouri, Indiana, and Ohio. However, the Woodmen refused to admit men from the larger cities in these states such as Chicago, Detroit, Milwaukee, St. Louis, and Cincinnati. They believed that more physically fit and wholesome members could be found in the small towns and farms of the Middle West.

Only white males between eighteen and forty-five could become beneficial members. The following categories of men were excluded:

> Railway brakeman, railway engineer, fireman, and switchman, miner employed underground, mine inspector, pit boss, professional rider and driver in races, employee in gunpowder factory, wholesaler or manufacturer of liquors, saloon keeper, saloon bartender, aeronaut, sailor on the lakes and seas, plough polisher, brass finisher, professional baseball player, professional football player, professional fireman, submarine operator, or soldier in regular army in time of war.

The chief symbols of the Modern Woodmen were the beetle, ax, and wedge. Local lodges were called Camps and members were known as Neighbors. By 1889 the lodge had signed up almost 40,000 members.

A serious dispute and rivalry between Root and the Head Physician of the Order, Dr. P. L. McKinnie of Moline, Illinois, precipitated a schism. The men leveled charges at each other and threatened law suits. To avoid further scandal the Head Camp deposed both men. Dr. McKinnie tried to establish a new society which never prospered. Root went to Omaha and set up the Sovereign Camp of the Woodmen of the World in 1890 and remained head of the new organization until his death in 1913. His new society employed many of the same lodge features and symbols as the Modern Woodmen; a Supreme Nest governed local Groves. In recent years the Woodmen of the World has become simply a life insurance society.

The Modern Woodmen of the World continued without founder Root and has also dispensed with much of the apparatus of a secret society. The ritual now makes no provision for an altar, Bible, prayers, chaplain, or burial service. A new member may skip the initiation and lodge meetings if he just wants to purchase life insurance. The Modern Woodmen of America enrolls about 426,000 men. Their female relatives may join the Royal Neighbors auxiliary.

(See **Royal Neighbors**)

PART III

Selected Bibliography

Acker, J. W., *Strange Altars* (St. Louis: Concordia, 1959).

Alexander, Charles C., *The Ku Klux Klan in the Southwest* (Lexington, Ky.: University of Kentucky Press, 1965).

Anderson, James, *The Constitution of the Free-Masons* (London, 1723 and 1738).

Baird's Manual of American College Fraternities, 17 ed. (Menasha, Wis.: Geo. Banta, 1963).

Box, Hubert S., *The Nature of Freemasonry* (London: Augustine Press, 1952).

Brown, Harvey Newton, *Freemasonry Among Negroes and Whites in America* (El Paso, Texas, 1965).

Cerza, Alphonse, *Anti-Masonry* (Fulton, Mo.: Missouri Lodge of Research, 1962).

Chalmers, David M., *Hooded Americanism: The First Century of the Ku Klux Klan* (Garden City, N. Y.: Doubleday, 1965).

Coil, Henry Wilson, *Coil's Masonic Encyclopedia* (New York: Macoy, 1961).

Daraul, Arkon, *A History of Secret Societies* (New York: Citadel, 1961).

Ferguson, Charles W., *Fifty Million Brothers* (New York: Farrar & Rinehart, 1937).

Gillette, Paul J., and Tillinger, Eugene, *Inside Ku Klux Klan* (New York: Pyramid Books, 1965).

Gist, Noel P., *Secret Societies: A Cultural Study of Fraternalism in the United States* (Columbia, Mo.: University of Missouri Studies, Vol. XV, October 1, 1940, No. 4).

Graebner, Theodore, *A Handbook of Organizations* (St. Louis: Concordia, 1948).

Hannah, Walton, *Darkness Visible* (London: Augustine Press, 1952).

———— *Christian by Degrees* (London: Augustine Press, 1954).

Jones, Bernard E., *Freemason's Guide and Compendium* (London: George G. Harrap, 1950).

Lee, Alfred McClung, *Fraternities Without Brotherhood* (Boston: Beacon, 1955).

Lewis, H. Spencer, *Rosicrucian Questions and Answers* (San Jose, Calif.: Supreme Grand Lodge of AMORC, 1959).

Macdonald, Fergus, *The Catholic Church and the Secret Societies in the United States* (New York: United States Catholic Historical Society, 1946).

Mackey, Albert, *Encyclopedia of Freemasonry* (New York: Masonic History Co., 1946).

Mellor, Alec, *Our Separated Brethren, The Freemasons* (London: George G. Harrap, 1964).

Pick, Fred L., and Knight, G. Norman, *The Pocket History of Freemasonry* (New York: Philosophical Library, 1953).

Preuss, Arthur, *A Dictionary of Secret and Other Societies* (St. Louis: B. Herder, 1924).

Quigley, Joseph A. M., *Condemned Societies* (Washington, D. C.: Catholic University of America, 1927).

Randel, William Peirce, *The Ku Klux Klan: A Century of Infamy* (Philadelphia: Chilton, 1965).

Reid, Ed, *Mafia,* rev. ed. (New York: Signet Books, 1964).

Schiavo, Giovanni, *The Truth About the Mafia* (New York and El Paso, Tex.: Vigo Press, 1962).

Statistics, Fraternal Societies 1964 (Indianapolis: Fraternal Monitor, 1964).

Stevens, Albert C., *Cyclopaedia of Fraternities* (New York: E. B. Treat, 1907).

Van Deventer, Fred, *Parade to Glory: The Story of the Shriners and Their Hospitals for Crippled Children* (New York: William Morrow, 1959).

Voorhis, Harold V. B., *Masonic Organizations and Allied Orders and Degrees* (Red Bank, N. J.: Henry Emmerson, 1952).

———— *The Eastern Star: The Evolution From a Rite to an Order* (New York: Macoy, 1954).

Webster, Nesta H., *Secret Societies and Subversive Movements* (London: Britons, 1955).

Whalen, William J., *Christianity and American Freemasonry* (Milwaukee: Bruce, 1958).

Williamson, Harry A., *The Prince Hall Primer* (Chicago: Ezra Cook, 1957).

Index

Acacia, 9 ff
Adoptive Masonry, 26
Ahepa, Order of, 12
Alhambra, Order of the, 12 ff
Amaranth, Order of, 14 f
AMORC, 138 ff
Ancient Arabic Order of Nobles of the Mystic Shrine, 55, 148 ff
Ancient Egyptian Arabic Order of Nobles of the Mystic Shrine, 116,
    154 f
Ancient Egyptian Order of Sciots, 148
Ancient Order of Foresters, 38
Ancient Order of Hibernians, 3, 69 ff
Ancient Order of Samaritans, 119
Anderson, James, 47
Animal lodges, 3, 23
Antlers, 37
Assemblies of God, 6
Attendance, lodge, 6

Benevolent and Protective Order of Does, 37
Benevolent and Protective Order of Elks, 31 ff
Birth of a Nation, 93
Black, Hugo, 97
Blackball, 4, 56, 81, 116
Blue lodges, 53 f
B'nai B'rith, v

Catholic Daughters of America, 82
Catholic Knights of America, 82
Catholic Knights of St. George, 82
Catholic Order of Foresters, 2, 15 f
Catholic Women's Benevolent Legion, 82
Catholic Workman, 16 f
Christian Cynosure, 64
Christian Reformed Church, 6, 36
Church of the Brethren, 6
Church of Jesus Christ of Latter-day Saints, v, vi, 7, 48
Church of the Nazarene, 6
Clansman, The, 93
Clement XII, 63
College fraternities, 1, 3, 40 ff
Colored Knights of Pythias, 116
Columbian Squires, 77
Commission on Fraternal Organizations, Lutheran Church-Missouri
    Synod, 36, 128, 131
Communist Party, v, 32, 50
Cosa Nostra, 100 ff
Czech Catholic Union of Texas, 82

165

Improved Order of Red Men, 133 ff
Independent Order of Foresters, 38
Independent Order of Good Samaritans, 68
Independent Order of Odd Fellows, 2 f, 116 ff, 134
Initiation rites, 5 f
International Concatenated Order of Hoo Hoo, 3
International Order of Good Templars, 4, 7, 66 ff
International Order of Twelve, 117
Invisible Empire, 4, 91 ff

Jehovah's Witnesses, 7
Job's Daughters, 7, 30, 72 ff
John Birch Society, v
John J. Jones Affiliation, 115
Johnson, Lyndon B., 52, 100
Junior Order Princes of Syracuse, 87
Junior Order United American Mechanics, 4, 74 ff, 126

Kappa Alpha, 43
Kappa Alpha Theta, 43
Kefauver investigation, 103 f
Kelley, Oliver Hudson, 108 f
Kennedy, John F., 23, 52, 72
Knights and Daughters of Tabor, 117
Knights of Columbus, 2 f, 4, 13, 46, 65, 76 ff
Knights of the Golden Eagle, 82 f
Knights of Malta, 3, 7, 83
Knights of Peter Claver, 84
Knights of Pythias, 7, 84 ff
Knights of Pythias of North and South America, Europe, Asia and
    Africa, 86, 116
Knights of St. John, 82
Knights Templar, 1, 55
Ku Klux Klan, 1 f, 7, 91 ff

Ladies Catholic Benevolent Association, 82
Ladies of the Golden Eagle, 83
Ladies Orange Benevolent Association, 127
Ladies' Oriental Shrine of North America, 154
Land, Frank S., 17
Lee, Alfred McClung, 42
Leo XIII, 63
Lewis, H. Spencer, 141 f
Lithuanian Roman Catholic Alliance of America, 82
Loyal Orange Association of British America, 3, 7, 125 ff
Loyal Order of Moose, 104 ff
Loyal True Blue Association, 127
Lutheran Church-Missouri Synod, 6, 10, 36, 108, 113

McDevitt, John, 65, 82
Mackey, Albert, 26, 62